"The Lord Is My Shepherd"

and Other Papers

Hamilton Smith

Scripture Truth Publications

"THE LORD IS MY SHEPHERD"

The Love that will not let me go was first published in *Scripture Truth* Volume 20, 1928, pages 28-31

The Disciple whom Jesus loved was first published in *Scripture Truth* Volume 20, 1928, pages 104-107

Copyright © 1928 Hamilton Smith/Central Bible Truth Depôt

First edition © 1987 Central Bible Hammond Trust Limited, Wooler
ISBN: 978-0-901860-06-4

Transferred to Digital Printing 2020

Revised edition (re-typeset, incorporating corrections and supplementary references) © 2020 Scripture Truth Publications
ISBN: 978-0-9511515-5-6

A publication of Scripture Truth

All rights reserved. No part of this publication may be reproduced, stored in a retrieval system, or transmitted, in any form or by any means, electronic, mechanical, photocopying, recording or otherwise without prior permission of Scripture Truth Publications.

Scripture quotations, unless otherwise indicated, are taken from The Authorized (King James) Version. Rights in the Authorized Version are vested in the Crown. Reproduced by permission of the Crown's patentee, Cambridge University Press.

Scripture quotations marked (N.Tr.) are taken from "The Holy Scriptures, a New Translation from the Original Languages" by J. N. Darby (G Morrish, 1890).

Scripture quotations marked (R.V.) are taken from "The Holy Bible containing the Old and New Testaments translated out of the original tongues : being the version set forth A.D. 1611 compared with the most ancient authorities and revised". Oxford: University Press, 1885.

Cover photograph ©iStockphoto.com/iacon (Jeffery Borchert)

Published by Scripture Truth Publications
31-33 Glover Street, Crewe, Cheshire, CW1 3LD

Scripture Truth is an imprint of Central Bible Hammond Trust, a charitable trust

We are grateful to Samuel Ford for his work in checking the text and Scripture references, and locating the origin of quotations from works by other authors.

Typesetting by John Rice

"THE LORD IS MY SHEPHERD"

FOREWORD

Each of the papers included in this collection is presented in the structured manner which was characteristic of Hamilton Smith's ministry. He lists the topics to be covered in each paper in an introduction, as sub-headings, or in the conclusion. For consistency, in preparing this new edition the author's topic titles are used as sub-headings throughout.

In preparing the text for publication some further Scripture references have been added, because not all today are as familiar with the Bible as Hamilton Smith's generation. These are enclosed in curly brackets {}.

Sources of prose and poetry quoted have been identified where possible, and these have been added in footnotes.

We trust you may find comfort, challenge, and encouragement as you read.

John Rice
August 2020

"THE LORD IS MY SHEPHERD"

"THE LORD IS MY SHEPHERD"

CONTENTS

Foreword 3
"The Lord Is My Shepherd" 9
   Our daily needs 12
   Our spiritual needs 12
   Our failure and dullness of soul 13
   The shadow of death 14
   The presence of enemies 14
   The daily round 15
   The prospect of eternity 15
The love that will not let me go 17
   The Awakening of Love 18
   The Maintenance of Love 19
   The Deepening of Love 21
The Disciple whom Jesus loved 25
   The Upper Room 27
   The Cross 29
   The Resurrection 29
   The Sea of Tiberias 30
   "When They Had Dined" 30
"One Thing" 34
   "One Thing Thou Lackest" 34
   "One Thing is Needful" 38
   "One Thing I Do" 40

THE LOVELINESS OF CHRIST 44
   A life of dependence and confidence 45
   A life of wholehearted subjection 47
   A life of lowliness 47
   A life of separation from evil 48
   A life finding its present and future portion in the Lord 49
   A life guided by the counsel of the Lord 49
   A life with the Lord as its one Object 50
   A life of secret joy and gladness 50
   A life lived in the light of the glory 51

SEVEN EXHORTATIONS 54
   "Stand fast in the Lord" 54
   "Be of the same mind in the Lord" 55
   "Rejoice in the Lord always" 56
   "Let your gentleness be known of all men. The Lord [is] near" 57
   "Be careful for nothing" 59
   "Think on these things" 60
   "Those things, which ye have both learned, and received, and heard, and seen in me, do: and the God of peace shall be with you" 61

CHRISTIAN EXPERIENCE 63
   Christ our Life 65
   Christ our Pattern 66
   Christ our Object 67

"THE LORD IS MY SHEPHERD"

Christ our Hope 68
Christ our Strength 69
THE GARDEN OF THE LORD 72
  The garden enclosed 75
  A watered garden 77
  A fruitful garden 78
  A fragrant garden 78
  A refreshing garden 79
"ABIDE IN ME" 82
  Fruit-bearing lives 84
  Answered prayers 85
  Christ-like walk 85
  Consistent ways 86
  Preserved from lawlessness 87
EPISTLES OF CHRIST 90
  Christ Written on the Heart 92
  Christ Manifested to All Men 93
  Christ The Object in Glory 95
IN HIS STEPS 100
  "His Steps" 101
  "Learn of Me" 105
AT HIS FEET 109
  At His Feet as a Learner 110
  At His Feet as a Mourner 113
  At His Feet as a Worshipper 115

"THE LORD IS MY SHEPHERD"

THE LORD THY KEEPER 120
   He will keep us from all danger 121
   His care will be unceasing 122
   His help is always available 123
   He will keep us at all seasons 124
   He will keep us from all evil 124
   He will keep us in all circumstances 125
   He will keep us through all time for evermore . . .126
THE BROKENHEARTED 128
   The Brokenhearted Sinner 129
   The Brokenhearted Saint .131
   The Brokenhearted Widow 133
   The Brokenhearted Saviour 134

"The Lord Is My Shepherd"

READ PSALM 23

> He knows His sheep;
>   He counts them and He calleth them by name.
> He goes before;
>   They follow as He leads, through flood or flame.[1]

The Twenty-third Psalm unfolds before us the blessings of one who takes his journey, through this world, with the Lord Jesus as his Shepherd.

The Psalm is closely connected with the preceding Psalm, as well as the one that follows. All three Psalms are of outstanding beauty and value, seeing that in each one Christ is the great theme. Psalm 22 presents the Lord Jesus as the Holy Victim offering Himself without spot to God, on the cross, in order to meet the holiness of God and secure His sheep. Psalm 23 presents the Lord Jesus as the Shepherd leading His sheep through a wilderness world. Psalm 24 presents the Lord Jesus as the King — the LORD of hosts — bringing His people into the kingdom glory.

The Psalm opens with the great statement, "The LORD is my Shepherd". Every believer can say, "The Lord is my

---

[1] H. Bonar, 1906

"THE LORD IS MY SHEPHERD"

Saviour"; but have we all definitely submitted to His leading, so that we can each say, "The LORD is my Shepherd"? He has told us that He is "*the* Shepherd" {John 10:11}; but have we each told Him, Thou art "*my* Shepherd"? Have we not only accepted Him as our Saviour who has died for us to save us from our sins, but also submitted to Him as our Shepherd to lead us home through all our difficulties?

Let us think for a moment of a flock of sheep *without a shepherd*. They are needy, foolish, weak, and timid creatures. If left to themselves to take their way through a wilderness scene, what would happen? Being hungry creatures they would soon starve; being foolish, they would wander and lose their way; being weak, they would grow weary and fall by the way; and being timid, they would flee before the wolf and be scattered.

In contrast, let us ask, "What will happen if the sheep take their journey under *the guidance of the shepherd?*" Now, if the sheep are hungry, the shepherd is there to guide them into green pastures; are they foolish, he is there to keep their wandering feet; are they weak, the shepherd is present to gently lead his sheep and carry the lambs; are they timid, he is in front to lead them through the rough valleys, and defend them from every foe.

Plainly, in a flock without the shepherd everything depends upon the sheep, and this must lead to disaster. It is equally plain, that if the shepherd goes before, and the sheep follow, it will mean a safe journey for the sheep with manifold blessing by the way.

This, indeed, is the picture that truly represents the journey of the Christian flock through this world; for does not the Lord, Himself, say that He is "the Shepherd of the sheep," that "He calleth His own sheep by name," that

"THE LORD IS MY SHEPHERD"

"He goeth before them, and the sheep follow Him; for they know His voice" (John 10:2-4).

The Twenty-third Psalm sets before us this blessedness of the Shepherd going before, and the sheep following. We, alas! in our self-confidence, may at times get in front of the Shepherd; or, growing careless, we may lag far behind. But granted the two conditions — that the Shepherd leads the way, and we follow — we can count upon the support of the Shepherd in every difficulty that we have to meet.

The Psalmist touches upon seven different circumstances that we may be called to face:

1. Our daily needs.
2. Our spiritual needs.
3. Our failure and dullness of soul.
4. The shadow of death.
5. The presence of enemies.
6. The daily round.
7. The prospect of eternity.

All these things may, in varied ways and at different times, cross our paths, and, if left to face them in our own strength, will surely overwhelm us with dread and disaster. Nevertheless, with the Lord as our Shepherd, to lead the way, we can with confidence face the journey that leads to glory, in spite of the difficulties that may lie in the path.

As every blessing in the Psalm flows from the first great statement, "The LORD is my Shepherd," we may very well preface each verse with these words, "The LORD is my Shepherd."

"THE LORD IS MY SHEPHERD"

OUR DAILY NEEDS

First (verse 1), there are *the daily needs of the body.* How are they to be met? The Psalmist does not say, "I hold a good office, I shall not want"; or, "I have kind friends who will care for me, I shall not want"; or, "I have ample means, I shall not want"; or, "I have youth, and health, and abilities, I shall not want."

In all these ways, and many others, the LORD may meet our wants, but of none of these means does the Psalmist speak. He looks beyond all second causes, and providential ways, and he sees the LORD; and with the LORD going before, and he himself following, he can say, "The LORD is my Shepherd; I shall not want."

OUR SPIRITUAL NEEDS

Secondly (verse 2), in the wilderness path there are not only temporal wants, but *spiritual needs.* For the Christian the world around is an empty wilderness. There is nothing in all its passing vanities to feed the soul. Its pastures are dry and barren; its waters, only waters of strife. If "the LORD is my Shepherd," He will lead me into His green pastures and beside the still waters.

How quickly the pleasures of this world pall, even upon its votaries. The spiritual food provided by the Shepherd is ever fresh, for He leads into the "*green* pastures." Moreover, the Shepherd not only feeds, but satisfies, for He makes His sheep to "*lie down* in green pastures." No hungry sheep would lie down in the midst of plenty. It would first feed, and when full lie down. Furthermore, the Shepherd leads beside the still waters. The waters of the stream that makes most noise, and show, are ever where the rocks are most abundant and the waters shallow. The still waters are quiet but deep. The Shepherd can calm our souls, and quench our spiritual thirst with the deep things

"THE LORD IS MY SHEPHERD"

of God far removed from the noisy and shallow strifes that occupy men and too often distract the Christian.

OUR FAILURE AND DULLNESS OF SOUL

Thirdly (verse 3), as we pass through this wilderness world we may *fail* in following the Shepherd; and, apart from actual failure, we may *grow weary* in the way and dull in our affections. Even so, if "the LORD is my Shepherd", "He restoreth," or "reviveth," my soul. Let us, however, remember it is "He," Himself, that "restoreth." It almost seems, at times, as if we think that when we have grown weary of our wanderings, we can restore ourselves by our efforts and in our own time. It is not so. We can wander; He alone can restore. Naomi, restored from her wandering in the land of Moab, can say, "I went out," but, she adds, "the LORD hath brought me home again" {Ruth 1:21}. She says, as it were, "I did the going out, but the LORD did the bringing back." Blessed be His Name, He can, and He does, restore. Were it not so, the people of God on earth would be little more than a great company of backsliders.

Moreover, He does not only restore, but having restored, He leads us into "the paths of righteousness for His name's sake." Alas! how often we may even in sincerity and zeal turn aside into paths of self-will, that are inconsistent with His Name, only to prove how little, in practice, we allow the LORD to lead us as our Shepherd. The path of righteousness, in which He leads, is a "narrow way" {Matthew 7:14} in which there is no room for the self-confidence of the flesh, and can only be trodden as we have the LORD as our Shepherd before us. Even so an Apostle found, when with real sincerity and zeal, and yet with great self-confidence, he said, "Lord, I am ready to go with thee, both into prison, and to death" {Luke 22:33}.

THE SHADOW OF DEATH

Fourthly (verse 4), we have to face "*the valley of the shadow of death.*" Even if we are alive and remain until the coming of the Lord, and have not personally to pass through death, yet, again and again, we have to face that dark valley as, one by one, our loved ones are taken from us. Then, in a wider sense, what is our passage through this world but a journey through the valley of the shadow of death? For, over all there sounds the toll of the passing bell.

Nevertheless, if the LORD is our Shepherd, we can say with the Psalmist, "I will fear no evil: for Thou art with me." The Lord can say, "If a man keep my saying, he shall never see death" (John 8:51). The Lord does not say, he will not pass through it, but he shall not see it. Those who stand round the death-bed of a dying saint may indeed see death, but the one that is actually stepping down into the dark valley sees JESUS. Even so, if we have to pass that way it is only passing "through." And the journey through is very short; for is it not written, "Absent from the body ... present with the Lord" {2 Corinthians 5:8}? And in that passage through the valley, not only is the Lord with us, but He is present with His rod and His staff — the rod to drive off every foe, the staff to support us in all our weakness.

THE PRESENCE OF ENEMIES

Fifthly (verse 5), in this wilderness world we are surrounded by *enemies* that would rob us of the enjoyment of our blessings, and hinder our spiritual progress. But the LORD is our Shepherd who prepares a feast for us in the very presence of our enemies. And not only so, He prepares His people for the feast, for He anoints the head with oil, and not only fills the cup, but makes it run over. He does a great deal more for us than

"THE LORD IS MY SHEPHERD"

ever we did for Him in the days of His flesh; for, though one of the Pharisees desired Him that He would eat with him, and in wonderful grace the Lord sat down to meat in the Pharisee's house, yet, He has to say, "My head with oil thou didst not anoint" {Luke 7:46}.

THE DAILY ROUND

Sixthly (verse 6), there is the *daily path* that we have to tread "all the days" of our lives. Each day of our life brings its ceaseless round of duties, difficulties, and circumstances, small and great. But if we follow the Shepherd we shall find that "goodness and mercy" will follow us. Were we nearer the Lord, following hard after the Shepherd, should we not with clearer vision trace His hand in the little things of the daily life, and discover therein His goodness and mercy?

THE PROSPECT OF ETERNITY

Seventhly, and lastly, looking beyond the days of our life into the great eternity that stretches beyond we see that if the LORD is our Shepherd, it is, not only to lead us through the wilderness, but, at last to bring us home to "dwell in the house of the LORD for ever." For the Christian it is the Father's house; there to *dwell* beyond all bodily wants, with every spiritual longing met, where no failure can intrude, no hearts grow cold, no shadow of death can come, no enemy approach, but where, indeed, the cup will run over. "The days of my life" will end "in the house of the LORD for ever." In that great home gathering not one of His sheep will be missing. "Those that Thou gavest Me I have kept, and none of them is lost" (John 17:12). Long years ago the saintly Rutherford wrote, "What think ye of His love? What of these feet that went up and down the world to seek His Father's lost sheep, pierced with nails? The eyes that were oft lift up to heaven unto God in prayer, wearied with tears? His head pierced with thorns? The face that is fairer than the sun, all maimed, and the hair pulled out of His cheeks? ... He took shame and gave you glory. He took the curse, and gave you the blessing, He took death, and gave you life^2... As the Chief Shepherd, He shall make an account of all His lambs, and tell His Father, these be all My sheep. I went through woods and waters, and briers, and thorns, to gather them in, and My feet were pricked and My hands and My side pierced, ere I could get a grip of them; but now here they are."[3]

Remembering all that He has done for us in the past, when, as the Good Shepherd, He gave His life for the sheep; knowing all that He will yet do for us when He comes as the Chief Shepherd, we may look up into His face during our present wilderness journey and say,

"THE LORD IS MY SHEPHERD."

> We follow in His footsteps;
> What if our feet be torn?
> Where He has marked the pathway
> All hail the briar and thorn.[4]

---

[2] Samuel Rutherford, *A Cry from the Dead*, from the Flower of the Church of Scotland, or an Exhortation at a Communion to a Scot's Congregation in London {about 1643}, from a Manuscript never before printed, Glasgow: 1765; reprinted in *Fourteen Communion Sermons by the Rev. Samuel Rutherford with a Preface and Notes by Rev. Andrew A. Bonar, D.D.*, Glasgow: Charles Glass & Co., 1876.

[3] Samuel Rutherford, *Sermon XI Canticles 2:14-17* Christ and the Dove, Christ and the Dove's Heavenly Salutations, with their pleasant conference together; or a Sermon before the Communion in Anwoth, 1630; *Fourteen Communion Sermons by the Rev. Samuel Rutherford with a Preface and Notes by Rev. Andrew A. Bonar, D.D.*, Glasgow: Charles Glass & Co., 1876.

[4] G. Ter Steegen, translated by E. F. Bevan, 1894

The love that will not let me go[5]

How blessed to have found in Christ a Friend who loves with a love that will not let us go, according to that Word which tells us, "Having loved His own which were in the world, He loved them unto the end" {John 13:1}.

Such love — the everlasting love of Christ, that never gives us up — cannot be satisfied until it has drawn out our love in response to His love. The answer to His love will only be realised in its fulness when at last we have reached love's eternal home. Nevertheless, on the way to the home, the love that appreciates Christ, in the place of His rejection and the day of His rejection, is very sweet to His heart. This we may surely learn from the value that is set by the Lord on the love of Mary, that led her to anoint His feet with the very precious ointment.

Very encouraging it is, and good for our souls, to learn the gracious ways of the Lord with His people in order to awaken love, maintain love, and deepen love, in our hearts. It is these gracious ways of the Lord that we would briefly trace in the New Testament stories of two devoted women.

---
[5] Extracted from *Scripture Truth* magazine, Volume 20, 1928, pages 28-31.

The Awakening of Love
Read Luke 7:36-39, 47

In the great scene that takes place in the house of Simon the Pharisee, we see the awakening of love for the Saviour in the heart of a sinner. The Lord, in the perfection of His way, had stooped to grace with His presence the feast which the Pharisee had spread. While sitting at the table an unbidden guest enters, of whom the Lord can say, "she loved much." How, we may ask, was this love awakened in her soul?

There is no question as to the character of the woman. The Spirit of God has described her as "a woman in the city, which was a sinner." Moreover, her bad reputation was well known, for Simon is also aware that "she is a sinner." She was a sinner and knew it, and Simon knew it and everyone knew it. Further, she was a *burdened* sinner, and possibly had heard those wonderful words of the Lord, "Come unto Me, all ye that labour and are heavy laden, and I will give you rest" {Matthew 11:28}. Be this as it may, it is beyond question that she saw in Christ the grace that could bless the undeserving. Thus driven by her need, and drawn by His grace, with the boldness of faith, she enters the Pharisee's house and takes her stand at the feet of Jesus.

The Spirit of God calls attention to the fine scene that follows with a "Behold." He would arrest our attention and have us to turn aside and see this great sight — the meeting between the devil's hell-bound sinner and God's heaven-sent Saviour. Doubtless, the onlookers were struck dumb with amazement, as they watched the scene unfolding itself before their eyes. They might well question what would happen. Would the Lord expose her character, condemn her sins, and dismiss her from His holy presence? Ah, no! The proud Pharisee may condemn the sinner, to find himself exposed by the Saviour; but the Lord will not condemn a confessed sinner.

The wisdom of His way is as perfect as the grace of His heart. At first no word is spoken. The guests are silent in wonder, the Lord is silent in grace, the woman is silent in sorrow. No sound breaks the silence but the sobs of a weeping sinner. If, however, nothing is said, much takes place, for the sinner's *heart was broken* and the sinner's *heart was won*. She "stood at His feet behind Him weeping" and she "kissed His feet". The tears tell of a heart that is broken, and the kisses of a heart that is won.

What was it that broke her heart and won her heart? Was it not that she saw something of the grace and holiness of the Saviour, and in the light of His glory she realised, as never before, the sinfulness of her life and her heart, and this *broke her heart*? But more, she realised that though she was a sinner full of sin, yet He was a Saviour full of grace for one who was full of sin. She found herself in the presence of One who knew her vile life through and through, and yet loved her, and this *won her heart*.

Good for each one, if we, too, have been in His presence, burdened and wretched by reason of our sins, there to discover that in Him we have found One who knows the worst about us and yet loves us. Thus to have love for Christ awakened in our souls, as we sing,

> I've found a Friend, oh, such a Friend,
> Who loved me ere I knew Him;
> Who drew me with the cords of love,
> And thus has bound me to Him.[6]

THE MAINTENANCE OF LOVE
READ LUKE 10:38-42

We have seen how love for Christ is awakened, and blessed indeed when at the outset of the Christian life the

---
[6] J. G. Small, 1863

heart is won for Christ. We have now to learn how the heart, in which love has been awakened, can be maintained in the freshness of first love.

Do we not all know that, with the passing of time, many things may creep in between the soul and Christ? Not always gross things, which indeed might arrest the soul by the very wretchedness they bring, but things that are small and apparently harmless — "the little foxes, that spoil the vines," and render the life unfruitful {Song of Songs 2:15}. The allowance of these little things will cast a chill over the affections, and gradually form an icy crust over the heart, and the Lord has to say to us, "Thou hast left thy first love" {Revelation 2:4}. Thus from one cause and another we often see, while love to Christ has been truly awakened in souls, some make little progress in spiritual intelligence whereas others grow in deeper acquaintance with the Lord and His mind. How, then, is the love, that has been awakened, to be maintained?

Will not the home at Bethany supply the answer? In the two sisters we have two saints in whom love to Christ has been truly awakened; yet in one sister we see a believer growing in grace and the knowledge of the Lord Jesus, while in the other sister we see a saint who is hindered by self and hampered by her service.

Martha's love was shown by seeking to meet the physical necessities of the Lord as a Man. Mary's love was seen in seeking to gratify the deep longings of His heart by hearing His word.

Martha was occupied with the "many things" which all have their end in death. Mary was occupied with the "one thing" that death could not take from her {Luke 10:41-42}. One has said, "No attention, even to Himself in the flesh, though it were from one that loved Him and whom

He loved, could replace this. The 'many things' end only in disappointment and death, instead of leading into life eternal, as did the words of Jesus, issuing from a heart broken that it might let forth the stream of life."[7]

If, then, we would know how *love is awakened*, we must in spirit visit the home of Simon; but would we know how *love is maintained*, let us visit the house at Bethany. Standing at the feet of the Saviour, in the house of Simon, love was awakened in the heart of a sinner; sitting at the feet of the Master, in the home of Martha, love was maintained. At His feet we are in His company; in His company we hear His words, and His words declare His heart. There we are learners in the school of love. How much do we know of the good part chosen by Mary — the turning aside from the busy round of life, and the activities of service to be alone with Jesus, and more, to draw nigh to Jesus for the love of being near Him? The Lord loves our company; He delights to have us in His presence. He may dispense with our busy service, but He cannot do without ourselves. Thus only will first love be maintained, and, if lost, be regained. We cannot live on the past. Past experiences may have awakened love, but only present communion can maintain love.

THE DEEPENING OF LOVE
READ JOHN 11

Passing now to another incident in the story of Mary of Bethany, we shall learn another lesson in the story of love. If in Luke 10 we have seen how love is *maintained* in the common round of life, in John 11 we shall learn how love is *deepened* in the sorrows of life. There life was flowing in its usual channel, here the everyday life is arrested by a great sorrow. Sickness has invaded the Bethany circle, and the shadow of death is creeping over the home. In the trial

---
[7] J. N. Darby, 1859

that has overtaken them how will the sisters act? Moved by grace they take the best possible course. *They draw upon the love of Christ.* In Luke 10 Mary is learning the love of Christ in the calm of a quiet life; in John 11 she is drawing upon that love amidst the storms of life. There she enjoyed His love in His company; here she uses His love in her sorrow. All this is writ plainly in the appeal that these devoted women make to the Lord. They send to Him saying, "He whom Thou lovest is sick" (verse 3). How brightly the faith and confidence in the Lord of these two sisters shines out in this brief message. They turn to the right Person, for "they sent unto *Him*." They use the right plea, for they say "Lord, behold, he whom *Thou lovest* is sick." They plead, not the feeble love of Lazarus for the Lord, but the perfect and unfailing love of the Lord for Lazarus. So, too, they appeal to the Lord in the right way, for they do not suggest what the Lord shall do; they neither ask the Lord to heal, nor to come, nor even to speak a word on their behalf. They simply spread out their sorrow before the Lord and cast themselves upon the boundless resources of unbounded love. Will love disappoint them? Ah, no! For love delights to respond to the appeal of hearts moved by love.

However, love divine will take its perfect way. A way indeed that to mere nature may seem passing strange. The sisters have delighted His heart by drawing upon His love; now He will delight their hearts by deepening in their souls the sense of His love, and thus deepening their love for Him. For it is ever thus, the deeper the sense of His love, the deeper will be the response of our love. "We love Him, because He first loved us" {1 John 4:19}.

To accomplish His gracious work He will use the sorrows of life, and, that His love may be deepened in their souls, He will first deepen the sorrow. The saints are called to the glory of God after they have "suffered a while" (1 Peter 5:10); so, on our way to glory, we often catch some brighter rays of His glory after a time of suffering. It was thus with the sisters. They had to suffer awhile, for the Lord tarries, and no word comes from the Lord. The days are passing, Lazarus is sinking, the shadow of death is creeping over the home. At last death has come; Lazarus is dead. They have suffered awhile; they shall now see His glory — for "this sickness is not unto death, but for the glory of God, that the Son of God might be glorified thereby" {verse 4}. To sight it was for death, in reality death was being used to bring into display the glory of Christ and swell the triumph of His victory over death. To accomplish these great ends, how perfect the way He takes.

Human love, thinking only of the relief of the sick one, would have started at once for Bethany. Human prudence, thinking only of self, would never have gone, even as the disciples say, "Master, the Jews of late sought to stone Thee; and goest Thou thither again?" {verse 8}. The Lord, rising above human love, and human prudence, acts according to divine love moved by divine wisdom. "As for God, His way is perfect" {2 Samuel 22:31}.

After patience has had her perfect work, in love's due time, the Lord comes to the bereaved sisters at Bethany, and reveals the deep love of His heart, as He talks with them, and walks with them, and weeps with them. He is going to deepen their love by His words of love, and ways of love, and tears of love. What depths of love lie behind those sublime words, "Jesus wept" {verse 35}. It was a wonderful sight to see a sinner weeping in the presence of His love, but more wonderful to see the Saviour weeping in the presence of our sorrow. That we should weep because of our sins is a small wonder; that He should weep because of our sorrows is a great wonder — a wonder that discloses how near He came, and *how near He is* to a sorrowing saint.

Why, we may ask, these tears? The Jews, standing round the grave, misinterpret the tears, for they say, "Behold how He loved him!" {verse 36}. Truly, the Lord loved Lazarus, but the tears were not the expression of His love for Lazarus. The sisters may weep for the loss of their brother; there was, however, no need for the Lord to weep for one He was about to raise. It was not for the dead He wept, but for the living — not for the loss of Lazarus, but for the sorrow of Mary and Martha. In a little, love will raise Lazarus, but first love will weep with Martha and Mary. He broke His heart to bind up our hearts, and shed His tears to dry our tears. In so doing He declared His love and deepens our love. Thus He uses the trials, the sorrows, and the rough ways of life to unfold the treasures of His love, and draw out our love to Him.

After this great trial the sisters would surely have said, "We knew that He loved us, but, until the trial came, we never knew that He loved us so much as to walk with us and weep with us in the trial."

At His feet, in Luke 10, Mary was learning His love; in John 11 she draws upon the love of which she had learned, and is deepened in the love that she draws upon.

What holy happy lessons can we learn from these different scenes. We learn that at the feet of Jesus, as sinners, love is awakened; at the feet of Jesus, as learners, love is maintained; and at the feet of Jesus, in our sorrows, love is deepened.

The Disciple whom Jesus loved[8]

Every true believer loves the Lord. Peter, speaking of the Lord to believers, can say, "Whom having not seen, ye love" {1 Peter 1:8}. In the presence of the proud Pharisee, the Lord can say of the woman who kissed His feet, "She loved much" {Luke 7:47}. Thus Scripture recognises this love and the Lord delights in it. Moreover, love for the Lord carries with it the promise of many blessings, not the least being the special realisation of the presence of the Lord and of the Father (John 14:21-24).

Yet Scripture recognises that love for the Lord may be found in very varied measures in different disciples on different occasions. The love of Mary of Bethany, who anointed the Lord with the "very precious ointment," was surely greater than that of the indignant disciples who said, "To what purpose is this waste?" {Matthew 26:7-8}. The love of Mary of Magdala, who "stood without at the sepulchre weeping," exceeded, on that occasion, the love of the disciples who "went away again unto their own home" {John 20:10-11}.

---

[8] Extracted from *Scripture Truth* magazine, Volume 20, 1928, pages 104-107.

Moreover, our love may wax and wane. Under pressure the love of many may "wax cold" {Matthew 24:12}. In the presence of the allurements of the world, this love may become dim, as in the case of a believer of whom the Apostle Paul can say, he "hath forsaken me, having loved this present world" {2 Timothy 4:10}.

Thus while love to the Lord is very precious in His sight and to be cherished and desired by the believer, yet, it is clear, we cannot trust in a love that is so liable to change. The love that we alone can rest in must be the love that knows no change — the love that abides — the love of Christ for His own.

"Our souls thro' many changes go:
His love no change can ever know."[9]

It is the realisation and enjoyment of the love of Christ that awakens our love to Him. "We love Him," says the apostle, "because He first loved us" {1 John 4:19}. Hence our love to Christ will be according to the measure in which we realise His love to us. Would we then love the Lord with more singleness of heart, let us not turn in upon our own hearts and think of our love to Him, but seek to delight our souls in His love to us.

The effect of the soul thus delighting itself in the love of Christ is blessedly set forth in connection with the Apostle John, in the closing scenes of the Lord's life. While, in contrast, the same scenes depict the sorrowful effects of confidence in our love to the Lord, in the case of the Apostle Peter. Both disciples loved the Lord with a true and deep affection beyond that of most, for it led them to leave all and follow Him. One disciple, however, trusted in his love to the Lord, while the other rested in the Lord's love to him. This is the outstanding difference between

---

[9] W. Hammond, 1745

THE DISCIPLE WHOM JESUS LOVED

these two men, so often found in close association in these last scenes.

When the Lord, in His wonderful grace, washes the disciples' feet, Peter can ask, "Lord, dost Thou wash my feet?" And when he learns that without the feet-washing there can be no part with Christ, immediately he exclaims with a glow of ardent love, "Not my feet only, but also my hands and my head" {John 13:6-9}. A little later, with genuine love to the Lord, he can say, "I am ready to go with Thee, both into prison, and to death"; and again, "Though all men shall be offended because of Thee, yet will I never be offended" {Luke 22:33, Matthew 26:33}. Then, at the betrayal scene, Peter, in his ardent love for the Lord, drew his sword in defence of his Master. Thus, both by words and deeds, he seems to say, "I am the man that loves the Lord." In contrast to Peter, the Apostle John says, as it were, "I am the man that the Lord loves," for five times, in these last scenes, he describes himself as "the disciple whom Jesus loved." Blessed, indeed, that His love should have so wrought with us that we should love Him, but far more wonderful that He should love us. In this wonderful love John delighted, and on this boundless love he rested.

THE UPPER ROOM
READ JOHN 13:21-25

The first occasion on which John is called "the disciple whom Jesus loved" is in the Upper Room, as described in John 13. What a scene it is for the heart to contemplate! Jesus is there with a love that can never break down, for "having loved His own which were in the world, He loved them unto the end" {John 13:1}. John is there delighting himself in the love of Christ, resting his head on the bosom of Jesus, and describing himself as the disciple whom Jesus loved. Peter is there with real and ardent love for the Lord, but trusting in his own love to the Lord rather than resting in the Lord's love to him. Lastly, Judas is there, with no love to the Lord — with the bag at his side and the devil in his heart, ready to betray the Lord and pass into the long dark night.

In Jesus we see how very near His love has brought Him to men like ourselves, inasmuch as John can rest his head on the bosom of the One who dwelt in the bosom of the Father. In John we see what the heart of the Saviour can do for a sinner, bringing him to perfect rest in perfect love. In Judas we see what the heart of the sinner can do with the Saviour — betray Him, with every profession of love, for thirty pieces of silver.

The feet washing is over and the time has come for the Lord to utter His farewell words; but for the moment His spirit is troubled by the presence of the betrayer. The Lord unburdens His heart to His disciples, saying, "One of you shall betray Me." Immediately the disciples look one on another, doubting of whom He spake. Looking one on another will never solve difficulties that arise amongst believers. We must look to the Lord, but looking to the Lord demands nearness to the Lord, and in the circle of the Upper Room, the disciple who was nearest to the Lord, was the one whose feet had been in the hands of the Lord, whose head was resting on the bosom of the Lord, and whose heart was delighting in the love of the Lord, who can describe himself as "one of His disciples, whom Jesus loved." Peter, the man who was trusting in his love to the Lord, was not near enough to the Lord to learn His mind, he must needs beckon to John.

Thus we learn that nearness to the Lord and intimacy with the Lord, is the happy portion of the one who is resting upon the Lord's love.

THE DISCIPLE WHOM JESUS LOVED

THE CROSS

READ JOHN 19:25-27

The second occasion on which John is described as the disciple whom Jesus loved, brings us to the cross. The mother of Jesus is present with other devoted women, and one disciple is there — the disciple whom Jesus loved. Where is now the disciple that rested in his love to Christ? Alas, away in some lonely spot with a broken heart, weeping tears of bitter shame. Where is the disciple who rests in the love of Christ? As at the Upper Room, so now at the cross, as near to Christ as he can be. And what is the result? He becomes a vessel fit and meet for the Master's use. The mother of Jesus is committed to his care. Resting in the Lord's love fits for service.

THE RESURRECTION

READ JOHN 20:1-4

For the third time, John is presented as the disciple whom Jesus loved on the resurrection morning, and again is found in association with Peter. The two disciples, learning from the women that the sepulchre is empty, hasten to the tomb. Then follows the record of what might appear to be insignificant detail, namely that Peter starts first, that both disciples run together, and finally that the disciple whom Jesus loved did outrun Peter. Nothing that the Spirit of God has recorded can be unimportant, though, as in this case, it may be difficult to seize the import of a particular incident. Yet, if we may be allowed to spiritualise this scene, we may learn, what is surely true, that while the man of ardent nature may often take the lead in some spiritual enterprise, it is the man who is leaning on the love of the Lord that finally takes the lead.

The Sea of Tiberias
Read John 21:1-7

In this instructive scene Peter and John again have a prominent place, and for the fourth time John is referred to as the disciple whom Jesus loved (verse 7). As usual the energetic and impulsive Peter takes the lead. He goes back to his old occupation. He does not ask others to do so, but simply says, "I go a fishing." However, under the influence of his dominating personality, "They say unto him, we also go with thee" {verse 3}. They went forth, therefore, and toiled all night, and for their pains caught nothing.

When the morning came, "Jesus stood on the shore: but the disciples knew not that it was Jesus" {verse 4}. Having by a question shown them the uselessness of efforts put forth *without His direction*, He proceeds to show how rich the results when acting under His control. Immediately the disciple whom Jesus loved perceives, "It is the Lord" {verse 7}. The one who is trusting in the Lord's love is the one who has quick spiritual perception.

"When They Had Dined"
Read John 21:15-22

Following upon the scene at the lakeside, the disciples find when they come to land, a fire of coals, fish laid thereon and bread, and an invitation to come and dine. Rich provision had been made for their needs, apart from all their efforts.

When they had dined we have the closing scene in which again Peter and John have a special place, and for the fifth time John is described as "the disciple whom Jesus loved" (verse 20). First we have the Lord's tender dealings with the man that trusted in his own love. Peter, who had said he was ready to go with the Lord to prison and death, had found that he was not ready to stand before the simple question of a serving maid. But of the actual denial, no word is said in this touching scene. The solemn breakdown had been dealt with between the Lord and His servant in an interview with which no stranger shall intermeddle. All we know of that interview is the statement of the Eleven, "The Lord is risen indeed, and hath appeared to Simon," confirmed long after by the Apostle Paul, when he wrote to the Corinthians that the risen Christ "was seen of Cephas, *then* of the twelve" {Luke 24:34; 1 Corinthians 15:5}. Wonderful love that with tender mercy gave the first interview to the most failing disciple.

If, however, in the first interview his conscience was relieved, in this scene his heart is restored. There the Lord had dealt with the outward failure, here He deals with the inward root that caused the failure. The root was confidence in his love to Christ, and the threefold question thoroughly exposes this root. It is as if the Lord said, "After all that has happened, do you still maintain, Peter, that you love Me *more than these?*" With the second question, the Lord says nothing of the other disciples: it is simply now, "Lovest thou Me?" With the third question, the Lord, using a different word, asks, "Art thou attached to Me?" {verse 17, N.Tr.}. By his third answer Peter puts himself entirely into the Lord's hands, saying, "Lord, thou knowest all things; Thou knowest that I am attached to Thee" {verse 17, N.Tr.}. It is as if Peter said, "I cannot trust my love, or talk of my love, or what I will do, but Lord, You know all things, and You know my heart, I will leave You to estimate my love, and tell me what to do."

No longer is Peter telling the Lord in self-confidence what he is ready to do, but it is the Lord, in infinite grace, telling His restored disciple what He will enable him to do. The Lord, as it were, says, "You no longer trust in your love to do great things for Me, you have left it to *Me*; then go forth and

- 'Feed My sheep' (verse 17),
- 'Glorify God' (verse 19), and
- 'Follow Me' (v. 19)."

The Lord seems to say, "Time was when you thought you loved Me more than these other disciples, now go forth and show your love by feeding My sheep that I love. You thought to glorify yourself above others by prison and death, now go forth to prison and death to glorify God, and when all is over down here, still *follow Me* far into the depths of glory where I am going." May we not say that not the least wonderful of all the wonders of the Lord's life, is the way He takes with a failing disciple?

But what of John? "Peter, turning about, seeth the disciple whom Jesus loved *following*." The man who trusted in his own love and had broken down, needed restoring grace, and the exhortation, "Follow Me." Not so the man who was resting in the love of the Lord, for he was "following."

Thus, in the disciple whom Jesus loved, we see set forth the blessed results that follow for those who rest in the love of the Lord; such:

- Dwell in nearness to, and intimacy with, the Lord;
- Are ready to be used in the service of the Lord;
- Will make spiritual progress;
- Will have spiritual discernment; and
- Will follow close to the Lord.

May it be our happy portion, like the bride of the Song, to say, "I am my Beloved's, and His desire is toward me" {Song of Songs 7:10}. If we can say little of our love to Him, we can safely boast of His love to us. It is the privilege of the youngest believer to say, "I am a disciple that Jesus loves," and the oldest and most advanced disciple can say nothing greater, for all blessing is found in His all-embracing love, that led Him to die for us that we too might go forth, in our small way, and feed His sheep, glorify God, and follow Him into the glory where He has gone.

"One Thing"

"One thing thou lackest" (Mark 10:21)

"One thing is needful" (Luke 10:42)

"One thing I do" (Philippians 3:13)

The Scriptures in which these three statements occur, bring before us very different characters. In the first passage we learn that "one thing" was lacking in the rich young ruler. In the second, we learn in the story of Martha and Mary that the "one thing" lacking is the "one thing" needful. In the third Scripture, we find that the "one thing" needful, is the "one thing" that marked the Apostle Paul.

Seeing that our Lord lays such stress upon this "one thing," it surely behoves us to search our hearts, in the light of these Scriptures, with the earnest desire to be marked by this "one thing."

"ONE THING THOU LACKEST"
READ MARK 10:17-22

In the story of the rich young ruler two truths come prominently before us. First we learn that in many ways our lives may be excellent, and yet lack "one thing."

"ONE THING"

Secondly, we discover that this "one thing" is single-hearted devotedness to Christ.

Of all the different characters that came in contact with our Lord, in His earthly course, none, perhaps, presents a more sorrowful end than that of this rich young ruler. There was so much at the commencement of his story that gave promise to a bright future as a disciple of Christ; yet, in the end, we read he "went away grieved." As far as we have any record, in Scripture, he is never again found in the company of Christ and His own. Therefore, even if at heart a believer, he missed the blessing of the company of Christ in the midst of His people, and failed as a witness for Christ in the world.

This young man was marked by many creature excellencies and much moral beauty. He was an earnest young man, for we read, he came "running" to the Lord. He was reverential for he "kneeled" in His presence. He had a desire after spiritual blessings, such as eternal life. His outward life was blameless, for he had observed the outward law from his youth. All these qualities, in their place, are beautiful and attractive, and the Lord was not unmindful of these creature excellencies, for we read, "Jesus beholding him loved him." Yet, with all these excellencies, the Lord discerns there was "one thing" lacking.

To make manifest the one thing lacking in his life the Lord applies three tests. As with the young man, so with ourselves, we may be living outwardly decent and blameless lives, and yet, our witness for Christ be marred by the lack of "one thing." It will be well therefore to prove ourselves by the three tests that the Lord sets before the ruler.

- First, he was tested by his earthly possessions;
- Secondly, he was tested by the cross;
- Thirdly, he was tested by a Person — the rejected Christ.

There was something he was asked to give up; something to take up; and Someone to follow.

The first test is *earthly possessions*. Taking them in the widest sense as all those things which would be an advantage to us as living in the world, we may ask, "Have we weighed up all these things in the light of Christ, and counted them but loss for Christ?" Have we reckoned up the advantages that birth may confer; the ease and worldly pleasures that riches can secure; the position, the honour, and dignities that intellect, or genius, or accomplishments, may command? Then, without minimising these things, have we looked full in the face of Jesus — the One that is altogether lovely — and, seeing that He is incomparably greater than all these things, have we, in the power of affection for Christ, deliberately made the choice that Christ shall be our great Object, and not these things?

The second test is *the cross*. The Lord says to the young man, "take up the cross." Are we prepared to accept the place in relation to the world in which the cross has set us before God? The Apostle could say, "God forbid that I should glory, save in the cross of our Lord Jesus Christ, by whom the world is crucified unto me, and I unto the world" (Galatians 6:14). The cross stands between us and our sins, the old man, and judgment: but have we also seen that it stands between us and the world? If we take up the cross, not only is the world condemned for us, but we shall be utterly refused by the world.

"ONE THING"

The third test is a *rejected Christ*; for the Lord says to the young man, "follow Me." Are we prepared to identify ourselves with One who is hated and rejected by the world; One who was born in a stable and cradled in a manger; who, in His passage through this world, had not where to lay His head; who died an ignominious death upon a cross of shame, and was buried in a borrowed grave; One, who in resurrection was still found in company with a few poor fisher folk; One, who was, and still is, in the outside place of reproach? Are we prepared to "go forth... unto Him without the camp, bearing His reproach" {Hebrews 13:13}?

Thus the tests in that day, as well as this, are, "Can we give up earthly advantages, take a place outside the world, and follow Christ, the One who is in reproach?" These tests come to us as they came to the young man, and the question for each one is, "What answer shall we give?"

We can answer these tests in one of two ways. First, like the young man of whom we read he "went away grieved," we may turn back to the things of earth. He did not turn away in anger or hatred of Christ. He had no fault to find with Christ; but the world was too strong for him. Like Demas, of a later day, he loved this present world. Secondly, we may give an answer like Peter and the disciples, of whom we learn that they left all and followed Christ (verse 28).

The one thing the young man lacked was single-hearted devotedness to Christ. So he "went away." The disciples with all their ignorance, their weakness, and their many failures, were drawn to Christ in affection and so left all to follow Him.

How often, since that day, has the history of this young man been repeated. Is there anything sadder than to look back and remember how many young men made a good start, and seemed to promise well, but where are they today? In spite of excellencies such as earnestness, sincerity, and zeal, they turned back, if not to the gross world, to the corrupt religious world; and the reason is plain, they lacked the "one thing" — that single-hearted devotedness to Christ, that sets Christ before the soul as *the first and supreme Object of their life*. It may be they put themselves before Christ, or the need of souls before Christ, or the good of saints before Christ, or service before Christ, with the result that, in the end, they turned back to the things of earth. There is not sufficient power in the love of souls, the love of saints, or the desire to serve, to keep our feet in the narrow path. Only Christ, Himself, can hold us in the outside place of reproach, following hard after Him.

"One Thing is Needful"
Read Luke 10:38-42

Passing to the touching scene at Bethany, we find two devoted women, of whom one lacked the "one thing" needful, while the other chose "that good part."

Martha, like the rich young man of Mark 10, was characterised by much that was excellent. The house at Bethany, apparently, belonged to her, and she willingly opened her home to receive the Lord of glory. Then, not only was she hospitable, but she was a busy servant in the service of the Lord. There are "many things" to be done for the Lord in this world, and Martha was occupied with these "many things." Nevertheless, with all these excellencies she had overlooked "one thing" and she has to learn that the "one thing" she had overlooked, is the "one thing… needful." In result, she was cumbered with service, irritated with her sister, and complaining before the Lord. How truly Martha represents that large class of

"ONE THING"

Christians who, unconsciously to themselves, make their particular service their great object rather than the Lord Himself. Such would engage all others as helpers in their special service, and are irritated if left "to serve alone." Lacking the "one thing," they are careful and troubled about "many things."

How right and happy to put our homes and means at the disposal of the Lord, and to be occupied in His blessed service; and yet this scene warns us that it is possible for these activities to be first in our thoughts and affections, rather than the Lord Himself. If this is so, we lack the "one thing" needful — the single-hearted devotedness that puts Christ before all service.

Of Mary we read, she chose the "good part," and that "good part" was *part with Christ*. For her Christ was the supreme Object before all else, whether possessions, or service, or her sister. Having Christ as her one Object she escaped the restlessness, the care and trouble that marked her zealous sister. While Martha was "cumbered about much serving," Mary was calmly sitting at the feet of Jesus. When Martha came to the Lord with her complaining word, Mary "sat at Jesus' feet, and heard His word."

We are not left to form our spiritual judgment as to the differences between these two sisters, for we are plainly told that the Lord reproved Martha and commended Mary.

In making the Lord her Object, Mary had chosen the "good part" which will not be taken from her. Very soon we shall leave all earthly possessions; in yet a little, service and toil will be past, but for ever and ever Christ will be the Portion and Object of our souls. Mary chose the eternal portion in time; she made Him her one great

Object, and chose above all else to sit in His company. Other things may be taken away, but this will not be taken away. For as she chose to be with Him in time, so will she be with Him for all eternity.

Does then, this better choice — this "one thing... needful" — mean that Mary neglected service for the Lord? Scripture not only rebukes such a thought, but clearly shows that she not only served the Lord, but her service was stamped with the Lord's approval in a way that is unique above all other service before or since. Here the Lord says, "Mary hath chosen that *good part*." In the fine scene of Matthew 26, the Lord says, "she hath wrought a *good work* upon Me" {verse 10}. The one who chose the "good part," in due season does the "good work."

So high is the Lord's approval of this good work, that He says, "Wheresoever this gospel shall be preached in the whole world, there shall also this, that this woman hath done, be told for a memorial of her" (Matthew 26:10-13).

Let us then remember that the "good part" must precede the "good work." Only as Christ is our one Object will service, and all else, fall into its rightful place.

"One Thing I Do"
Read Philippians 3:13

Turning now to the third chapter of the Epistle to the Philippians we find in the Apostle one who, above all others, answered to the three tests that the Lord set before the rich young ruler. He gave up earthly possessions, he took up the cross, and he followed Christ.

First, what were the possessions that he gave up? Like the young ruler, Paul was marked by creature excellencies and worldly advantages in no small degree. He was well born, he was freeman of no mean city, he was highly educated,

"ONE THING"

he was intensely zealous in his religion, and as touching the law he was blameless.

All these circumstances and qualities combined to give him a great place in this world. But there came a day when, like the rich young man, he came in touch with Christ. Then came the test. Could he give up all that was an advantage to him as a man in this world — all those things which made something of Paul — in order that he might make everything of Christ? Let us remember that neither the rich young ruler, nor the "young man... whose name was Saul"{Acts 7:58}, was asked to give up the things of shame. All realise that we cannot follow Christ and go on with the hidden things of shame. Such things we are glad enough to leave behind. The test was, and is, can worldly advantages, human zeal, and blameless character, natural birth, religious reputation, be left behind *as an object* so that henceforth, instead of self, Christ may become the one Object of the life?

Instead of turning away grieved from Christ and going back to his great possessions, like the rich ruler, Paul forgot "those things which are behind" and reached forth unto Christ {Philippians 3:13}. He saw the glory of Christ, and he saw Christ in the glory. The rich ruler came in contact with Christ, but apparently, in spite of all His wonderful miracles he only saw in Christ a good Man; he did not see the glory of Christ. This made the great difference between these two young men. Paul saw the glory of Christ with the immediate result that all the glory of this world — all those things which were gain to him as a man in the flesh — were counted loss for Christ. He did not belittle these natural advantages: on the contrary, he reckoned them up, and having done so he counted them loss when compared with the glory of Christ. His natural excellencies were eclipsed by the "excellency of the knowledge of Christ Jesus" his Lord {Philippians 3:8}.

Secondly, there was not only what he gave up, but what he took up. In all truth he took up the cross. His one desire, as he passed through this world, was to be "made conformable unto His death" — the death of Christ {Philippians 3:10}. If Christ had died to the world, then Paul was done with the world. For Paul the cross not only ended himself as a man in the flesh, but it for ever closed to him this present evil world.

Thirdly, having given up all his natural advantages as the object of his life; having taken up the cross which closed the world, he followed Christ as the one Object of his life. He turned his back on all earthly religion; he went outside the camp unto Christ, bearing His reproach. Henceforth Christ was his one Object, for he can say:

- "For me to live is Christ" (Philippians 1:21);
- "That I may win Christ" (Philippians 3:8);
- "Be found in Him" (Philippians 3:9); and
- "That I may know Him" (Philippians 3:10).

Here, then, was a man who could say in all truth, the one thing that the ruler lacked, the "one thing" that Martha had to learn is needful, is the "ONE THING I DO." Henceforth his life was a life of single-hearted devotedness to Christ. For him Christ was the one supreme Object — not sinners, not saints, not service — but Christ. No one was ever more zealous in preaching the gospel of the grace of God to sinners, no one ever cared for all the Churches like the Apostle, no one was more untiring in service; but above all, and before all, Christ was his one Object. He did not lack the "one thing" like the ruler: he was not distracted by "many things" like Martha. He had before him one thing — to follow Christ. Thus it was he forgot

"ONE THING"

"those things which are behind" and reached forth unto "those things which are before" {Philippians 3:13}.

Moreover he lets us know what these things are. He shows us very clearly that they all centre in Christ.

- First, Christ in the glory (Philippians 2:9-10).
- Secondly, "the calling on high of God in Christ Jesus" (Philippians 3:14, N.Tr.).
- Thirdly, the coming of the Saviour, the Lord Jesus Christ (Philippians 3:20).
- Fourthly, being "fashioned like unto His glorious body" (Philippians 3:21).

How good then to make Christ our one Object. If we make service our object we shall end in seeking to exalt ourselves. If we make sinners our object we shall in all probability be drawn back into the world. If we make saints our object, they will break our hearts. But if Christ is our first and supreme Object we shall, like the Apostle, fight a good fight, finish the course, and keep the Faith, for Christ alone can hold our feet in the narrow path, guide us through every difficulty, and sustain us in the presence of every opposition. May we then in our little measure, be able to say with the Apostle, "One thing I do... I press toward the mark for the prize of the high calling of God in Christ Jesus" (Philippians 3:13-14).

> Morn, noon, and night,
> Thro' days o'ercast and bright,
>   My purpose still is one;
> I have one end in view,
> Only one thing I do,
>   Until my Object's won.[10]

---

[10] Anon., 19th Century; attributed to J N Darby in *"The Evangelist"* Volume III, 1869, edited by H H Snell

The Loveliness of Christ

READ PSALM 16

We need every Scripture for conviction, correction, and instruction; but the Scriptures that present "the things concerning Himself" must have a special charm for the Christian {Luke 24:27}. It is this that makes Psalm 16 so attractive, for it sets forth the moral perfections of Christ, the perfect Man, as He trod the path of life through this world of sin and death. How good, then, to look away from self, and the very best of our fellow-men, to contemplate this perfect Man in all His excellence — to sit down, as it were, under His shadow with great delight and find His fruit sweet to our taste.

It is reported of one, who listened to the ministry of the saintly Rutherford, that he said, "He showed me the loveliness of Christ."[11] In his Psalm we may surely say that David, led by the Spirit, unrolls before us the loveliness of Christ.

We know that Christ is a Divine Person — the Eternal Son and, as such, was the perfect manifestation of God to man. But we also know that He was a true Man — the Son of Man — and as such, was the perfect expression of

---

[11] An English merchant, about 1650

man before God. It is in this latter aspect that Christ is presented in this beautiful Psalm.

We can learn what God is only in Christ; and we can learn what man is in perfection only as set forth in Christ. In Him we see the beautiful qualities, the gracious experiences, the joy and the gladness, that mark the life of the perfect Man before God, together with the fulness of joy to which this life leads. Thus Christ becomes the only standard of excellence — the perfect model for the believer. Moreover, in being occupied with Christ there is a transforming power. Feeding upon Christ as the Bread of God which "cometh down from heaven" — to trace His path through this world in all its loveliness, will, in a special way, draw out our affections to Himself {John 6:33}. When here, the Father opened the heavens to express His delight in Christ; and He gives us to delight in the same Object in which He delights. Delighting our souls in Him we shall be changed into His likeness.

Here, then, we have portrayed in all its blessedness the inner life of a perfect Man lived before God by One who trod this path of life in perfection, and who has reached the end of the path — the right hand of God.

A LIFE OF DEPENDENCE AND CONFIDENCE

"Preserve me, O God: for in Thee do I put my trust" (verse 1).

This perfect life is a life of *dependence* and *confidence*. Dependence upon the power of God and confidence in the love of God. The Lord Jesus did not trust Himself or look to others — either men or angels — to be preserved from all the opposition and dangers He had to meet. Nor did He depend upon Himself, with entire dependence to God, saying, "Preserve me, O God"; and He did so with entire confidence, for He said, "In Thee do I put my trust." He was entirely dependent upon God's hand of power, because He had entire confidence in God's heart of love. With unbounded confidence in boundless love He looked to God to preserve Him.

He was neither ignorant of, nor indifferent to, His enemies. He could say, "They that hate Me without a cause are more than the hairs of Mine head: they that would destroy Me, being Mine enemies wrongfully, are mighty" (Psalm 69:4). He knew their number; He knew their strength; He knew their treachery; but He knew that God was above all His enemies, and that no one was above God, and in perfect confidence He looks alone to God. As He can say in the language of another Psalm, "As for Me, I will call upon God; and the LORD shall save Me. Evening, and morning, and at noon, will I pray, and cry aloud: and He shall hear My voice" (Psalm 55:16-17).

And yet, in the perfection of His way, He was at times brought very low in His circumstances, and thus tested in a way, and to an extent, that we shall never know. At times He had nowhere to lay His head, and on occasions lacks even a cup of cold water. But such testings only brought out the perfection of His Manhood, for still He can say, "Preserve Me, O God: for in Thee do I put My trust." And God answered His prayer, and used a fallen woman to quench His thirst, and some unknown person to provide a pillow for His head.

Following in the footsteps of the Lord, the Apostle Paul could say in his prison, "The Lord shall deliver me from every evil work, and will *preserve* me unto His heavenly kingdom" (2 Timothy 4:18). Have we such confidence in the love of the Father, and of Christ, that, in the presence of enemies, dangers, and desertion, we can say, "Preserve me, O God, for in Thee do I put my trust"?

A LIFE OF WHOLEHEARTED SUBJECTION

"O my soul, thou hast said unto the LORD, Thou art my Lord: my goodness extendeth not to Thee" (verse 2).

The perfect life is a life of wholehearted *subjection* to the will of God. As the perfectly subject Man He could say to Jehovah, "Thou art My Lord." Coming into the world He said, "Lo, I come to do Thy will, O God" (Hebrews 10:9). Passing through this world He could say, "I do always those things that please Him" (John 8:29). Going out of this world He said, "Father... not My will, but Thine, be done" (Luke 22:42).

Doing only the Father's will, all that He did was perfectly good. He "went about doing good" {Acts 10:38}. There was also Divine goodness toward man, perfectly expressed in the Son of God. But the goodness of which this Psalm speaks is the goodness of Christ as man towards men, and though perfect in its place, does not rise to the height of Divine goodness. So the Lord can say of this goodness, "My goodness extendeth not to Thee."

Only as we are subject to the Father's will shall we do good as we pass along our way. When converted, the first question asked by the Apostle Paul was, "What shall I do, Lord?" (Acts 22:10). Hitherto he had done his own will; now he submits to the will of the Lord. The proud, overbearing Pharisee becomes the lowly man in subjection to the Lord.

A LIFE OF LOWLINESS

"To the saints that are on the earth, and to the excellent thou hast said, In them is all my delight" (verse 3, N.Tr.).

This perfect life is a lowly life that finds its delight with God's poor people. The perfection of Jesus in all His lowly grace is seen in the place He takes in association with the poor of the earth. "Hath not God chosen the poor of this world rich in faith, and heirs of the kingdom which He hath promised to them that love Him?" (James 2:5).

Are believers lowly and of little account in this world? Then let them remember that the Lord delights to associate with such, for we read, "Though the LORD be high, yet hath He respect unto the lowly: but the proud He knoweth afar off" (Psalm 138:6). To indulge the pride of the flesh and boast in birth, and worldly position, is to separate ourselves from the excellent of the earth and put ourselves "afar off" from God. The word to each one is, "[Go] along with the lowly" (Romans 12:16, N.Tr.).

However feeble, however failing, however poor, they are the excellent of the earth, and in them God finds His delight. Are we lowly enough in our eyes, and have we so learnt our own nothingness that we can associate with God's poor people and find our delight where He finds His?

A LIFE OF SEPARATION FROM EVIL

> "Their sorrows shall be multiplied that hasten after another: their drink-offerings of blood will I not offer, and I will not take up their names into my lips" (verse 4, N.Tr.).

The life of the perfect Man is a life of separation from evil. The Lord refused every object that would come in between the soul and God. The devil bid high in the endeavour to turn the Lord from the separate path. He offered Him "all the kingdoms of the world" if He would but worship the devil. The Lord's reply was, "It is written, thou shalt worship the Lord thy God, and Him only shalt thou serve" (Luke 4:5-8). A very little bit of this world is too often sufficient to ensnare our souls, and thus we turn aside to seek some passing satisfaction in the things of this world, only to find that we multiply to ourselves sorrows.

The Lord refused the idols of this world. He would not take up their names into His lips. The word to us is, "Little children keep yourselves from idols" (1 John 5:21).

A LIFE FINDING ITS PRESENT AND FUTURE PORTION IN THE LORD

> "The LORD is the portion of mine inheritance and of my cup: thou maintainest my lot. The lines are fallen unto me in pleasant places; yea, I have a goodly heritage" (verses 5-6).

The LORD is the portion of this life and of the inheritance that lies outside this world. Not only was the Lord entirely separate from the world, but the LORD was His portion in another world. Moreover, as He passed along His way to the eternal inheritance the LORD filled His cup in His daily path. The cup is the actual present enjoyment of the future heavenly portion. With the LORD as His heavenly portion, as well as the source of His present joy, He can say, "The lines are fallen unto me in pleasant places; yea, I have a goodly heritage." As to circumstances, He was indeed the "man of sorrows, and acquainted with grief" {Isaiah 53:3}. It is not, however, the circumstances of which the Psalm speaks, but of *the inner life lived in the circumstances*. The life was lived in the sweet enjoyment of the love and support of the Father, and such experiences turned the roughest paths into "pleasant places."

In the dullness of our way we little realise what the joy of a life must be that is lived in relationship with the Father and the constant enjoyment of all that the Father is. We shall know the fulness of the joy of this life in a day to come; but the Lord Jesus knew it without a cloud as He trod the path of life through this world.

A LIFE GUIDED BY THE COUNSEL OF THE LORD

> "I will bless the LORD, who hath given me counsel: my reins also instruct me in the night seasons" (verse 7).

"THE LORD IS MY SHEPHERD"

This perfect life is a life in which the LORD is the Counsellor and Guide. It is written that, "It is not in man that walketh to direct his steps" (Jeremiah 10:23). And again we read, "In *all thy ways* acknowledge Him, and He shall direct thy paths" {Proverbs 3:6}. It is not merely that we refer to the Lord in some great emergency, but that we habitually wait upon the Lord in the details of life, great and small. Acknowledging Him, we shall find that He guides us: then shall we be able to say, "I will bless the LORD, who hath given me counsel."

A LIFE WITH THE LORD AS ITS ONE OBJECT

"I have set the LORD always before me: because He is at my right hand I, shall not be moved" (verse 8).

The perfect life has only one object — the Lord Himself. Christ walked on earth with singleness of eye. He set Jehovah before Him as His only object. In such a life there is nothing of self, and no room for self-will.

Setting the LORD before Him, he found the Lord was ever at hand to support Him. Moreover, being at His right hand to support, nothing moved Him from the path of life.

Such is the path open to the believer. Alas! we have to own how little we know of its blessedness; and yet, if day by day, we set the Lord before us as our one object: to serve Him, to please Him, to do His will, shall we not find that He will be at our right hand to support us? And being supported, we shall not be moved, or turned aside, by any trying circumstances, opposition, slights or sufferings we may be called to meet.

A LIFE OF SECRET JOY AND GLADNESS

"Therefore my heart is glad, and my glory rejoiceth: my flesh also shall rest in hope. For thou wilt not leave my soul in hell; neither wilt thou suffer thine Holy One to see corruption" (verses 9-10).

This perfect life has its joy and gladness, though not like the joy of this world that depends upon outward circumstances. The Lord says, "*My heart is glad*," not necessarily, My circumstances are bright. The joy is in the heart; even as David can say, "Thou hast put *gladness in my heart*, more than in the time that their corn and their wine increased" (Psalm 4:7). The world's joy is in prosperous circumstances, the corn and the wine. The Lord could say to His disciples, "These things have I spoken unto you, that my joy might remain *in you*" (John 15:11).

The Lord's joy remains even in view of death; for His confidence is still in God, "*Thou* wilt not leave my soul to Sheol, neither wilt *Thou* allow Thine Holy One to see corruption" {verse 10, N.Tr.}. Christ is indeed the "Holy One," but believers are "holy and beloved," and, as such, can know the blessedness of the life of Christ as man {Colossians 3:12}. They, too, can look on with confidence, knowing that God will not leave the soul in death nor the body in corruption.

A LIFE LIVED IN THE LIGHT OF THE GLORY

"Thou wilt show me the path of life: in thy presence is fulness of joy; at thy right hand there are pleasures for evermore" (verse 11).

This life is a life lived in the light of the glory to which it leads. Every path has a destined end. "The path of life" leads into the presence of the LORD where there is fulness of joy and pleasures for evermore. In all the opposition the Lord Jesus had to meet — the contradiction of sinners, the insults and reproach from the religious world, the ignorance and forsaking of His own — He endured in the light of the glory before Him. As we read, 'Who for the joy that was set before Him endured the cross, despising the shame, and is set down at the right hand of the throne of God." The word to us is, "Consider Him that endured such contradiction of sinners against Himself, lest ye be wearied and faint in your minds" {Hebrews 12:2-3}.

Alas! we often break down in the presence of contradiction and insult; we grow weary and faint under the pressure of a long, drawn-out trial, because we lose sight of the glory at the end of the road — the joy that is set before us. Instead of quietly enduring insults and shame, too often we return evil for evil, and railing for railing. We may attempt to justify our strong words and our hasty acts, but the one test is, would Jesus have acted as we did? Would Jesus have said what we said?

If then we would think and speak and act as the Lord Jesus did, when treading the path of life — if in any measure we would experience the blessedness of the lovely life marked out by Christ — let us tread the path, "*Looking unto Jesus*" in the glory — the end of the path; let us *"Consider" Jesus* as He trod the path of life {Hebrews 12:2-3}. Then it may be that the transforming power of the loveliness of Christ will, even now, change us into His image "from glory to glory" {2 Corinthians 3:18}.

Moreover, let us remember that the grace that enabled the Lord to tread the path of life is available for us; for, from His place in the glory, He still serves us as our great High Priest, to succour, sympathise, and sustain us as we seek to follow in His steps in the path of life that He has marked out for us. Whatever we may have to meet, whatever we may be called upon to endure — opposition, insults or desertions — let us remember the word, "Be strong in the *grace* that is in Christ Jesus" (2 Timothy 2:1).

Such is the loveliness of Christ as He trod the path of life, lived in all its beauty before God, and marked out for His people to follow. A life of dependence upon the Father's hand of power, confidence in the Father's heart of love, and subjection to the Father's will. A life of lowliness that finds its delight with God's poor people — the excellent of the earth. A life of separation from evil, finding in the Lord its future portion and its present cup of blessing. A life guided by the counsel of the Lord, and which has the Lord as its one Object, and has the Lord ever-present to support. A life of secret joy and gladness that ends at last in the presence of the Lord, where there is fulness of joy and pleasures for evermore.

> The Lord is Himself gone before;
>   He has marked out the path that we tread,
> It's as sure as the love we adore,
>   We have nothing to fear nor to dread.
>
> For the path where our Saviour is gone
>   Has led up to His Father and God,
> To the place where He's now on the throne,
>   And His strength shall be ours on the road.
>
> And with Him shall our rest be on high,
>   When in holiness bright we sit down,
> In the joy of His love ever nigh,
>   In the peace that His presence shall crown.[12]

---

[12] J. N. Darby, 1849

Seven Exhortations

READ PHILIPPIANS 4:1-9

The first nine verses of the fourth chapter of the Epistle to the Philippians bring before us the seven closing exhortations of the Epistle. These exhortations were never more important, and comforting, than in these last difficult days.

The day of grace draws to its close. Evils, within and without, oppose us. To meet these different trials we have the encouragement of these seven exhortations, which, if taken to heart and carried out, will lift us above the sorrows of the way and guide us through every trial.

"STAND FAST IN THE LORD" (VERSE 1)

This great exhortation brings before us our resource in the presence of every kind of opposition. When the Apostle gave us this word, he, himself, was in bonds — the prisoner of the Lord. Within the Christian circle he was opposed by jealous men who were even preaching Christ out of envy, strife, and contention seeking to "arouse tribulation" for him (Philippians 1:15-17, N.Tr.). Outside it adversaries were plotting for his life (Philippians 1:28).

Nevertheless, he is not cast down nor overcome by one or the other. Do professors seek to add to his afflictions by preaching out of envy? Then, at least, he can rejoice that Christ is preached. Do adversaries seek his life? He is not terrified.

What then sustained him, and enabled him to stand unshaken in the presence of every opposition? It was this, his confidence was entirely in the Lord — in a word, he stood fast in the Lord. And having experienced the sustaining grace and support of the Lord, he passes on the exhortation to the saints of all ages. In the presence of every opposition we may have to meet, he says, *"Stand fast in the Lord."*

The adversaries without, and the "envy", "strife", and "contention," within the Christian circle, that existed even in the Apostle's day, have increased on every hand in our day. Yet we have this comforting exhortation, "Stand fast in the Lord."

We are neither exhorted, nor expected, to stand fast in our own strength, or knowledge, or wisdom. We are to stand fast against every effort of the enemy to further break up and divide the people of God, whether from within or without, by standing fast in the strength of the Lord, the living Lord, who is exalted above every name, and is "able even to subdue all things unto Himself" (Philippians 2:9; 3:21).

"BE OF THE SAME MIND IN THE LORD" (VERSE 2)

Nothing is more distressing to the heart, and enfeebling to testimony, than the differences of judgment that exist among the true people of God. In the second chapter of the Epistle the Apostle traces all envy and strife to this one root — "Vainglory" (Philippians 2:3). Even in the very presence of the Lord, there was a strife among the Apostles because each wanted to be accounted the greatest (Luke 22:24). So, in the Apostle's day, there was strife, as the result of the vainglory of some who wanted to be great. And in our day, all the division and strife that has come in among the people of God can be traced to this one root — someone wanted to be great.

The vainglorious man will ever be an envious man — jealous of every one that is more spiritual or more gifted than himself. And jealousy expresses itself in malice, and malice ends in strife (James 3:14-16).

How, then, can we "be of the same mind in the Lord"? The Apostle clearly shows that this can only be as we are marked by "lowliness of mind," and, to have the lowly mind, he says, "Let this mind be in you, which was also in Christ Jesus" {Philippians 2:3, 5}. His was the lowly mind that led Him to make Himself of no reputation in order to serve others in love. Self likes to be served, and thinks it is exalted when being served by others; but love delights to serve.

If, then, we each forget self, refuse to seek a reputation for ourselves, and seek only to serve others in love, according to the lowly mind of Christ, we shall have the mind of the Lord, and *"be of the same mind in the Lord."*

"REJOICE IN THE LORD ALWAYS" (VERSE 4, N.TR.)

The Apostle has been telling us:

1. that within the Christian circle there are some marked by "envy", "strife", and "contention" {Philippians 1:15-16};

2. that "all seek their own, not the things which are Jesus Christ's" {2:21};

3. that many walk in such a way that they are "the enemies of the cross of Christ" {3:18}.

Alas! these things are still found among the people of God, and may well call forth sorrow and tears, even as they did with him.

But the Apostle tells us more; he not only looks abroad and sees the failure of the saints, but he looks up and sees the glory of Jesus. He sees Christ in the glory, "the prize of the calling on high" (Philippians 3:14, N.Tr.). He sees that God has called us to be with Christ and like Christ in glory, and he sees the blessed end of the wilderness journey with all its sorrows and failure. With this glorious end in view, he forgets the things that are behind and presses on to the goal.

Moreover he not only looks up to Christ in the glory, but he looks for the coming of the Lord Jesus Christ to change our bodies of humiliation into bodies of glory. Looking around he may weep, but looking up, and looking on, he rejoices, and exhorts us to *"Rejoice in the Lord always."*

We cannot rejoice in ourselves, our service, or our walk: we cannot always rejoice in our circumstances or in the saints. But with the living Christ on high, and the coming Christ before us, we can "Rejoice in the Lord always."

"LET YOUR GENTLENESS BE KNOWN OF ALL MEN. THE LORD [IS] NEAR" (VERSE 5, N.TR.)

It is only as we walk with the Lord before us, according to the first three exhortations, that we shall be able to carry out this exhortation which sets before us the character of gentleness by which we should be known of all men. Too often we are known for our self-assertiveness, for our strong opinions, and perhaps violence of expression, in relation to the affairs of this world. If our minds are set on things above we shall not be eager to assert ourselves in regard to things on earth. As to these matters we do well to yield to others and be reticent of asserting our opinions. Thus we shall wear the beautiful character of Christ who was marked by "meekness and gentleness" (2 Corinthians 10:1). We are to beware of being drawn into strife with those who may oppose, for "the servant of the Lord must not strive; but be gentle unto all men" (2 Timothy 2:24). Let us remember it is more important to exhibit the character of Christ, than to assert our opinions, even if right, or to defend ourselves. Men can oppose our opinions, our assertions, and our violence; but who can stand against gentleness? As one has said, "Gentleness is irresistible."[13]

Moreover, to encourage us to gentleness, the Apostle reminds us that "the Lord is near." There is no need for us to assert ourselves and seek to put the world right, for the coming of the Lord is near, and at His coming He will right every wrong.

May we not also say that, in another sense, the Lord is near to us, however little we may realise His presence. He hears and sees all that we say and do. How many a hard and violent word we may have uttered in unguarded moments that would never have been said had we realised His presence.

The disciples, in their hardness, rebuked the mothers who brought their little ones to Jesus. The Lord, in His gentleness said, "Suffer little children, and forbid them not, to come unto Me" {Matthew 19:14}. Again, the disciples, in their resentment against villagers that refused to receive the Lord, would, with violence, bring down fire from heaven to destroy them. The Lord, in His gentleness, utters no word against His rejectors, but quietly passes on to another village.

---

[13] H. Martyn, diary entry for September 20th 1806 in *Memoir of the Rev. Henry Martyn, B.D.*, London: J. Hatchard, 1819

May we then so speak and act while pursuing a separate path as the quiet in the land, that, if the world takes any account of us, it will only be to mark our "gentleness."

"BE CAREFUL FOR NOTHING" (VERSE 6)

Here the Apostle's exhortation has in view the circumstances of life. He is not unmindful that, in a world of sorrow and sickness, of want and care, there will be trials to face and burdens to be borne; but, he would not have us racking our poor hearts with them. He, himself, writes from a prison, and had suffered want, and a companion and fellow-labourer had been sick nigh unto death; but in these sorrowful circumstances he had been lifted above all anxious care, and therefore can say to others, "Be careful for nothing."

We may have to face trials in our families, trials in our businesses, trials amongst the Lord's people; sorrows from sickness, sorrows from want, sorrows from the saints, that press upon us as a great burden and, as one has said, "How often a burden possesses a person's mind, and when he tries in vain to cast it off, it comes back and worries him."[14]

How then can we find relief? How is it possible to "Be careful for nothing"? Very blessedly the Apostle unfolds the way to be free, not necessarily of the trial, but of *the burden* of the trial, so that it no longer weighs the spirit down with care and anxiety. He says, "In everything by prayer and supplication with thanksgiving let your requests be made known unto God" {verse 6}. Thus only shall we find relief. "In everything," whatever the trial may be, small or great, make it known to God in prayer; and tell God exactly what you wish, "let your requests be made known unto [Him]." The requests may not be for our good, they may not be according to the mind of God;

---

[14] J. N. Darby, *Collected Writings*, Volume 27, Philippians

they may even be foolish, but we are to make them known to God.

What will be the result? Will He answer the requests? Will He remove the trial? He may see that to answer the request, or remove the trial would not be for our good. So far as the immediate trial is concerned, He will act in perfect wisdom for our good, according to His perfect love. But this God will do; He will relieve our hearts *from the burden* of the trial. If we pour out our hearts before Him, He will pour in His peace into our hearts — that "peace of God which passeth all understanding" {verse 7}.

So Hannah found, in the days of old, when, in her sore trial she could say, "I... have poured out my soul before the Lord." In result, we read, "Her countenance was no more sad." And yet, at the time, her circumstances were just the same. Afterwards, indeed, the Lord changed her circumstances, but first He showed that He had the power to change Hannah. From grief of heart, and bitterness of soul she was brought into great peace — "the peace of God which passeth all understanding" — through making known her requests to God (1 Samuel 1:6-18).

"Think on these things" (verse 8)

Rejoicing in the Lord, and set free from care, we shall be able peacefully to delight our souls in the things that are pure and praiseworthy. In a world far from God we are continually faced with evil. It is in us and around us; it presses upon us from every side. At times we have to face it and deal with it in ourselves, or others; but, even so, to have to do with evil, in any form, is defiling, and soiling to the mind. Alas! there is often with us a tendency to pry into evil, and to be over-busy in contending against it!

God would have us to find our delight in all that is true, and noble, and just, and pure. The flesh in us is ever ready to listen to slander, and bad reports, and things that are vicious and blameworthy. But says the Apostle, listen to the good report, and if there is anything virtuous and praiseworthy in your brother, *"think on these things"*.

"THOSE THINGS, WHICH YE HAVE BOTH LEARNED, AND RECEIVED, AND HEARD, AND SEEN IN ME, DO: AND THE GOD OF PEACE SHALL BE WITH YOU" (VERSE 9)

The mind being set on things which are pure will prepare the way for a life that is according to God. Right "thinking" will lead to right "doing." Having said of the things that are pure, "*think* on these things," the Apostle now says, "Those things, which ye have… seen in me, *do*."

It is not enough to have "learned" and "received" the truth, through the Apostle's writings, or to have "heard" it from his lips and "seen" it in his life. What we have learned, and received, and heard, and seen, is to be translated into our lives. We are, as another Apostle has said, to be "*doers* of the word, and not hearers only" (James 1:22).

Then, says the Apostle, if our minds are set on things that are pure, and our lives in accordance with the truth — if we "think" and "do" rightly — we shall find that not only does the peace of God keep our hearts, but that the God of peace will be with us.

In spite then of all the failure of the Church and the trials by the way, how blessed the portion of those believers who—

- Stand fast in the Lord;
- Have the same mind in the Lord;
- Rejoice in the Lord;
- Are known of all men for their gentleness;
- Are careful for nothing;

- Have their minds set on things that are pure, and
- In practice, "do" the things they have learned and received.

Such will have their hearts governed by the peace of God, and will enjoy the support of the God of peace. In all these exhortations there is nothing that cannot be carried out by the simplest and youngest believer, in the power of the Holy Spirit. They demand no special gift; they require no great intellectual attainment. They form the very essence of practical Christian life, and are as applicable in these last difficult days as in the early days of freshness and power.

> Thus ever on through life we find,
> To trust, O Lord, is best,
> Who serve Thee with a quiet mind,
> Find in Thy service rest.
>
> Their outward troubles may not cease,
> But this their joy will be —
> Thou wilt keep him in perfect peace
> Whose mind is stayed on Thee.[15]

---

[15] J. S. B. Monsell, *Spiritual Songs for the Sundays and Holydays*, 2nd edition, London: John W Parker and Son, 1859

Christian Experience

The Epistle to the Philippians is the Epistle of Christian experience, for therein is presented in a very touching way the experience of a believer that lives the Christian life in the power of the Holy Spirit.

Though written by the Apostle Paul, he does not speak of his apostleship, nor does he address the Philippian Assembly as an Apostle, but as a servant of Jesus Christ. Nor does he speak of gifts and powers that alone belong to an Apostle, but rather of experiences that are possible for every Christian. Thus, as we read the Epistle, each one can say, "This is the experience that is possible for me to enjoy if I live the Christian life in the power of the Holy Spirit."

Moreover, the blessed experiences brought before us, are entirely independent of circumstances, be they bright or sad. When the Apostle wrote the Epistle his circumstances were sorrowful and heart breaking. He, himself, had been a prisoner four years. He knew that within the Christian circle there were some who were taking up the service of the Lord, and preaching Christ, even of envy and strife, supposing to add to his afflictions (Philippians 1:15-16); outside the Christian circle there were adversaries plotting for his life (1:28). Such was the state of the Christian profession, that he has to say, "All seek their own, not the things which are Jesus Christ's" (2:21); and the walk of many was so low that, instead of being witnesses to Christ and His work, they had become "enemies of the cross of Christ" {3:18}.

Such were the circumstances: Paul a prisoner; inside the Christian circle envy, strife, and contention; all seeking their own, and many walking as enemies of the cross; outside the Christian circle, adversaries, dogs, and evil workers.

Nevertheless, in the midst of these distressing circumstances the Apostle enjoys the most blessed Christian experience.

He has deep and continual *joy* in the Lord, and in everything that is of the Lord in the saints (3:1, 3; 4:4, 10).

His *confidence* is unshaken in the Lord. He boasts in Christ Jesus and has no confidence in the flesh (1:6; 3:3; 4:13).

He is kept in a *peace* that passeth all understanding (4:7).

His *love* flows out to the saints and appreciates their love to him (1:8; 4:1; 1:17).

His *hope* is undimmed as he looks for the Lord Jesus to come from heaven (3:20).

His *faith* trusts the Lord in whatsoever state he may be found (4:12-13).

What then is the secret of such blessed experiences in the midst of such distressing circumstances? In one word it is CHRIST. All the experiences that pass before us in the

Epistle are the result of a believer having Christ before the soul.

The Apostle sees clearly that Christ is in the presence of God to represent believers; and that believers are left here, for a time, to represent Christ. He sees that Christ is our righteousness before God and the prize at the end of the journey, and he has only Christ before him every step of the way. For him it was Christ, "whether it be by life, or death" {1:20}. Having Christ before him he enjoyed all the blessed experiences of which he speaks in the Epistle, and in order that we may enjoy these experiences he sets Christ before us.

> Firstly, CHRIST our Life (1:20-21).
>
> Secondly, CHRIST our Pattern (2:5).
>
> Thirdly, CHRIST in glory our Object (3:13-14).
>
> Fourthly, CHRIST our Hope (3:20-21).
>
> Fifthly, CHRIST our Strength (4:13).

CHRIST OUR LIFE
READ PHILIPPIANS 1:20-21

In all truth Paul could say, "For me to live is Christ." Christ was all in his life. If he lived it was by Christ and for Christ. If death was his portion, he would die for Christ. Over such a Christian adversaries had no power, Satan no point of attack, and death no terror. The malice of envious brethren could not move him, and the low walk of those who were minding earthly things only drew forth his tears. Self being gone as a motive, insults and desertions called forth no bitterness and rancour; circumstances, however trying, drew forth no complaint. His one object was not to defend or exalt himself, or to decry and belittle others, but, in all circumstances, whether in life or death, to magnify Christ.

Christ our Pattern
Read Philippians 2:3-5

In the second chapter of the Epistle, Christ is looked at, not as going up to glory, but, as coming down to the cross; and we see the lowly mind that marked Him in every step that led to the cross. Thus Christ, in all the lowly grace of His path from the glory to the cross, is presented as our perfect pattern to produce in us a life of lowly grace.

The flesh in us is vain-glorious; and the effort to exalt self often leads to the belittling of others. This vanity ever leads to strife. So we read of the disciples, "there was… a strife among them," because they each wanted to be accounted the greatest (Luke 22:24). And how often, since that day, the root of strife amongst the people of God has been that someone wanted to be great. But, says the Apostle, "Let nothing be done through strife or vain glory; but in lowliness of mind let each esteem other better than themselves." We may think this difficult at times, for as one has said, "We may see great vanity or pride in another, and one may be going on really better than this or that person;"[16] but if close to Christ, however comparatively well we may be walking, we shall feel in His presence our own nothingness, and see our brother in Christ, and all that is of Christ in him, rather than his faults. Then it will not be difficult for each to esteem other better than themselves.

The Apostle, then, would have us to be of one mind (verse 2); the one mind that he desires us to have is the lowly mind (verse 3); and the lowly mind has been perfectly set forth in Christ (verse 5). The mind of Christ would deliver us from all the self-importance of the flesh, and lead each to esteem himself the least of all.

---
[16] J. N. Darby, *Collected Writings*, Volume 27, Thoughts on Philippians 2

CHRISTIAN EXPERIENCE

We need the *mind* of Christ if we are to exhibit the lowly grace of Christ. It is possible to affect a lowly manner, and use humble words before men; but, if the grace of Christ is to be seen in us we shall need the lowly mind that was in Christ. Thus the Apostle turns our eyes upon Christ. Devoted saints may help us by their lives, their ministry, and their means, but only Christ can be the perfect pattern for the Christian's walk.

In all His perfect path He was the exact contrast to all that the flesh is. He made Himself of no reputation; the flesh in us would seek to make a reputation for itself, if not in the world, in the religious circle. He took upon Him the form of a servant; but the flesh in us likes to be served. He humbled Himself; the flesh in us likes to exalt itself. He was obedient to the will of another; we like to do our own wills.

In Christ we see the perfect love that made itself nothing in order to serve others. Love delights to serve; self likes to be served, and thinks itself exalted when others are waiting upon it. Walking in the spirit of Christ, vain glory would be gone, and the lowly grace of Christ would be expressed.

> Win lowliness of heart, and having won beware;
> And that thou grow not proud of lowliness have care.[17]

CHRIST OUR OBJECT
READ PHILIPPIANS 3:13-14

If the second chapter has brought Christ before us in His lowly path, as the pattern for our walk, the third chapter presents Christ in glory as the One to whom we are pressing on. God sets before us Christ in glory as the perfect Object of our souls, and tells us that we are called on high to be with Him and like Him. With this bright

---
[17] R. C. Trench, *A Century of Couplets*, 1835

prospect before us, we can forget the things that are behind, rise above the sorrows of the present, and reach forth to those things that are before.

In the light of the eternal glory that lies before us, present things lose their value, and the sorrows by the way are seen to be but for a moment. Compared with the coming glory the things which are gain in the flesh are counted by the Apostle not only as valueless, but as dung. Having seen their worthlessness, he not only leaves them behind, but, he forgets them. He says, as it were, "They are not worth talking about, even to condemn: I forget them" (verse 13).

Christ had laid hold of Paul for the express purpose of having the Apostle like Him and with Him in the glory, and Paul says, "The one thing I desire is to lay hold of Christ in glory — the prize that awaits me at the end of the journey."

Blessed for all believers to know, young and old, that if we have not yet laid hold of Christ in the glory, Christ has laid hold of us, and He which hath begun a good work will perform it unto the end. No matter how rough the road, how many the trials, how deep the sorrows, how powerful the enemy, Christ will not let us go. He is "able even to subdue all things unto Himself," so will at last have us like Him and with Him in the glory {verse 21}.

> And is it so! we shall be like Thy Son,
> Is this the grace which He for us has won?
> Father of glory, thought beyond all thought,
> In glory, to His own blest likeness brought.[18]

Christ our Hope
Read Philippians 3:20-21

The Apostle looks up to heaven and sees Christ in the glory, and realises that believers are going to be conformed

---

[18] J. N. Darby, 1872

to the image of His Son in glory. It is possible to walk as He walked and, in this sense to be morally like Christ even now, but, to be conformed to His image we must wait for the coming glory. We are still in these bodies of humiliation, subject to sickness, and want, and exposed to dangers, and death.

How then are we to be delivered from these bodies of humiliation? We look at Christ in heaven and we see we are going to be like Him: our conversation — the home of our affections — is in heaven, and to heaven we look for the change of these bodies. "From which also," writes the Apostle, "we await the Lord Jesus Christ [as] Saviour, who shall transform our body of humiliation into conformity to His body of glory" {verses 20-21, N.Tr.}.

Once, He came as Saviour to deliver us from our sins, and judgment, by His death on the cross. A second time He is coming as Saviour to deliver us from these bodies of humiliation.

One thing remains to effect this great change — the coming of Christ. Christ is our hope, and at His coming what we have looked forward to in hope will be accomplished in glory. In the twinkling of an eye we shall be like Christ and with Christ.

> One moment here, the next with Thee in bliss,
> Oh, what a glorious prospect, Lord is this!
> Changed in a moment, from the flesh set free,
> Caught up together with Thyself to be.[19]

CHRIST OUR STRENGTH
READ PHILIPPIANS 4:12-13

It is blessed to *look back* and see the grace of Christ in His lowly life. It is blessed to *look up*, and see Christ in the glory, as the one glorious Object before our souls. It is

---
[19] Anon.

blessed to *look on,* and see that Christ is coming to conform us to His image. Nevertheless, as we *look around* we are faced with the circumstances by the way — prosperous circumstances that may make us careless and self-satisfied, or trying circumstances by which we may be cast down and dissatisfied. How then can we be lifted above our circumstances, be they bright or sad?

To answer this question, the Apostle gives us his own experience. He had known what it was to be in want as well as in prosperity: he had been full, and he had hungered; he had enjoyed plenty and he had suffered need. But in all circumstances he had found his support in Christ. So he could write, "I have strength for all things in Him that gives me power" {verses 12-13, N.Tr.}.

In circumstances of weakness the Lord had said to him, "My grace is sufficient for thee: for my strength is made perfect in weakness" (2 Corinthians 12:9). Therefore Paul had learned, in whatsoever state he was, to be content.

That Christ was his strength, was not merely an absolute truth to which he assented, but a truth that he had learned by experience. Through the strength of Christ he was made superior to all circumstances, be they bright or sad.

We may say Christ can do this for all saints, and it is true. But Paul says, as it were, "*He has done it for me,* for I have learnt by experience that I can do all things through Christ which strengthened me" {verse 13}.

Thus, with Christ before his soul as his Life, his Pattern, his Object, his Hope, and his Strength, the Apostle entered into all the blessed experiences that are proper to a Christian in the power of the Holy Spirit, and this in spite of so much in his circumstances that was sorrowful and heart breaking.

Seeing that Christ remains, and that Christ is the Same (Hebrews 1:11-12), it is still possible, amidst the gathering gloom of these closing days, for the simplest believer to enjoy this same true Christian experience — this *joy* in the Lord, *confidence* in the Lord, *peace* in the midst of trials, *love* that flows out to the saints, *hope* that looks for the coming of Christ, and *faith* that counts upon His support to lift us above every trial by the way.

> Turn your eyes upon Jesus,
> Look full in His wonderful face:
> And the things of earth will grow strangely dim,
> In the light of His glory and grace.[20]

---

[20] H. H. Lemmel, 1918

The Garden of the Lord

A garden enclosed is my sister, [my] spouse;
A spring shut up, a fountain sealed.
Thy shoots are a paradise of pomegranates, with
    precious fruits;
Henna with spikenard plants;
Spikenard and saffron;
Calamus and cinnamon, with all trees of frankincense;
Myrrh and aloes, with all the chief spices:
A fountain in the gardens,
A well of living waters,
Which stream from Lebanon.
Awake, north wind, and come, [thou] south;
Blow upon my garden, [that] the spices thereof may
    flow forth.

Let my beloved come into his garden,
And eat its precious fruits.

I am come into my garden, my sister, [my] spouse;
I have gathered my myrrh with my spice;
I have eaten my honeycomb with my honey;
I have drunk my wine with my milk.
Eat, O friends; drink, yea, drink abundantly, beloved
    ones!

                    (Song of Songs 4:12 – 5:1, N.Tr.).

With these choice words from the Song of Songs, the Bridegroom likens His bride to a garden of delights. Probably, all believers, with hearts opened to understand the Scriptures, would agree that in the Bridegroom, or the "Beloved", of the Song of Songs, we have a beautiful figure of Christ. Most would also concede that, in the interpretation of the Song, the bride sets forth Christ's earthly people.

While, however, the strict interpretation of the bride has Christ's earthly people in view, we are surely warranted in making an application to the Church, the heavenly bride of Christ.

Furthermore, if we may discover in this garden the excellencies that Christ would find in His heavenly bride, do we not at the same time learn what the love of Christ is looking for *in the hearts* of those who compose the bride? May we then, for a little, meditate upon this garden, with its spring, its fruit, its spices, and its living waters, as describing what the Lord would have our hearts to be for Himself.

First, we notice that the Bridegroom always speaks of the garden as "My garden"; while the bride delights to own it as "His garden". "Awake, O north wind... blow upon *My* garden," says the Bridegroom. The bride replies, "Let my Beloved come into *His* garden." In response, the Bridegroom says, "I am come into *My* garden." The application is plain — the Lord claims our hearts for Himself. "My son, give Me thine heart," says the Preacher (Proverbs 23:26). "Sanctify the Lord God in your hearts," is the exhortation of an Apostle (1 Peter 3:15), and again, another Apostle can pray that "Christ may dwell in your hearts by faith" (Ephesians 3:17).

It is not simply our time, our means, our brains, and our busy service, that the Lord desires, but first, and above all, He claims our affections. We may give all our goods to the poor, and our bodies to be burned, but, without love it will profit nothing. The Lord is still saying to us, "Give Me thine heart."

"Thou hast left thy first love", was a solemn word indicating that whatever excellencies belonged to the believers thus addressed, their hearts had ceased to be a garden for the Lord {Revelation 2:4}. As one has said, "A wife may take care of the house, and fulfil all her duties so as to leave nothing undone for which her husband could find fault; but if her love for him has diminished, will all her service satisfy him if his love to her be the same as at first?"[21]

Above all, then, the Lord claims the undivided affection of our hearts. The garden must be His garden. Moreover, if the Lord claims our hearts to be a garden for His delight, they must have the marks of the garden that is according to His mind.

As we read this beautiful description of the garden of the Lord, we note five outstanding features which set forth in figure what the Lord would have our hearts to be for Himself. First, the garden of the Lord is an *enclosed* garden. Secondly, it is a *watered* garden, with its spring shut up and its fountain sealed. Thirdly, it is a *fruitful* garden — a paradise of pomegranates with precious fruits. Fourthly, it is a *fragrant* garden, with trees of frankincense, and all the chief spices. Lastly, it is a *refreshing* garden from whence "the living waters" flow, and the fragrance of its spices is carried to the world around.

---

[21] J. N. Darby, *Seven Lectures on the Prophetical Addresses to the Seven Churches*, 1852

THE GARDEN OF THE LORD

THE GARDEN ENCLOSED

If the heart is to be kept as a garden for the pleasure of the Lord, it must be as "a garden enclosed." This speaks of a heart separate from the world, preserved from evil, and set apart for the Lord.

May we not say that, in the Lord's last prayer, we learn the desire of His heart that His people should be as "a garden enclosed"? We hear Him tell the Father, that His own are a separate people, for He can say, "They are not of this world, even as I am not of the world". Again, He desires that they may be a preserved people, for He prays, "Keep them from the evil". Above all, He prays that they may be a sanctified people, for He says, "Sanctify them through Thy truth" (John 17:14-17).

Does not the Preacher exhort us to keep our hearts as "a garden enclosed", when he says, "Keep thy heart more than anything that is guarded"? (Proverbs 4:23, N.Tr.). Again we do well to heed the Lord's own words, "Let your loins be [girdled] about" {Luke 12:35}. Unless the girdle of truth holds in our affections and thoughts, how quickly our minds will be drawn away by the things of this world, and the heart cease to be "a garden enclosed".

Again, the Apostle James desires that our hearts may be preserved from evil, when he warns us, "If ye have bitter envying and strife *in your hearts*, glory not, and lie not against the truth ... for where envying and strife is, there is confusion and every evil work" (James 3:14-16). Never has there been a scene of confusion and strife amongst the people of God that has not had its hidden root, of envy and strife, in the heart. We may be sure that the heart that entertains bitterness, envying, and strife, will be no garden for the Lord.

How necessary, then, to have our hearts kept in separation from the world, and preserved from evil. Nevertheless, the refusal of the world, and the flesh, will not be enough to constitute our hearts "a garden enclosed." The Lord desires that our hearts may be sanctified, or set apart for His pleasure, by being occupied with the truth and all that is according to Christ. Does not the Apostle Paul set before the Philippians "a garden enclosed" — a heart sanctified for the Lord, when he says, "Whatsoever things are true, whatsoever things are honest, whatsoever things are just, whatsoever things are pure, whatsoever things are lovely, whatsoever things are of good report; if there be any virtue and if there be any praise, *think on these things*" {Philippians 4:8}?

If the heart is full of cares, fretting over wrongs, and full of bitterness towards those who may have acted badly towards us: if we are entertaining evil imaginations, malicious thoughts, and revengeful feelings towards a brother, it is very certain our hearts will be no garden for the Lord.

If then we would have our hearts freed from things that defile and turn the heart into a barren waste, choking the garden with weeds, let us follow the instruction of the Apostle when he tells us, "Be careful for nothing; but in everything by prayer and supplication with thanksgiving let your requests be made known unto God" {4:6}. Having, like Hannah of old, poured out our hearts before the Lord, and unburdened our minds of all the cares, the sorrows, and the trials that pressed upon our spirits, we shall find that "the peace of God, which passeth all understanding, shall keep your hearts and minds through Christ Jesus" {4:7}. Thus set free from all that might come in between the soul and God, our hearts will be at liberty to enjoy the things of Christ, and our minds free to "think on these things" — these holy and pure things which should mark one whose heart is "a garden enclosed".

A WATERED GARDEN

The heart that is set apart for the Lord will have its hidden source of refreshment and joy. It will be a garden with "a spring shut up" and "a fountain sealed". A spring is an unfailing supply; a fountain rises up to its source. The Prophet can say, of one who walks according to the mind of the LORD, that his soul shall be "like a watered garden, and like a spring of water, whose waters fail not" (Isaiah 58:11). To the woman of Sychar the Lord spoke of giving "a fountain of water, springing up into eternal life", to be *"in"* the believer {John 4:14, N.Tr.}. The world is entirely dependent upon surrounding circumstances for its passing joy; the believer has a spring of joy within — the hidden life lived in the power of the Holy Spirit.

As the Spring of life the Holy Spirit meets all our spiritual needs by guiding us into "all truth": as the Fountain of life, He engages our hearts with Christ above {John 16:13}. The Lord can say, "the Spirit of truth, which proceedeth from the Father, He shall testify of Me" — Christ in His new place in the glory {John 15:26}. Thus as the Spring, He refreshes our souls with the truth; as the Fountain springing up to its source, He engages our hearts with Christ.

Let us, however, remember that the spring, which is the source of blessing, is "a spring *shut up*", and the fountain is "a fountain *sealed*". Does this not remind us that the source of blessing in the believer is sealed to this world, and wholly apart from the flesh? The Lord speaks of the Comforter as One that "the world cannot receive, because it seeth Him not, neither knoweth Him: but ye know Him; for He dwelleth with you, and shall be in you" (John 14:17). Again we read, "the flesh lusteth against the

Spirit, and the Spirit against the flesh: and these are contrary the one to the other" (Galatians 5:17).

Alas! we may mind the things of the flesh, and turn aside to the world, only to find we grieve the Spirit so that our hearts, instead of being as a watered garden, become but a dry and barren waste.

A FRUITFUL GARDEN

The "spring" and the "fountain" will turn the garden of the Lord into a fruitful garden — "a paradise of pomegranates with precious fruits". The ungrieved Spirit will produce in our hearts "the fruit of the Spirit", which, the Apostle tells us, "is love, joy, peace, long-suffering, kindness, goodness, fidelity, meekness", and "self-control" (Galatians 5:22-23, N.Tr.). What, indeed, are these precious fruits of the Spirit but the reproduction of the character of Christ in the believer? The fountain, rising up to its source, occupies with Christ and His excellencies; and, "beholding... the glory of the Lord" we "are changed into the same image from glory to glory" {2 Corinthians 3:18}. Thus the heart becomes a garden of the Lord bearing precious fruit for the delight of His heart.

A FRAGRANT GARDEN

Not only is the garden of the Lord a garden of precious fruits, but a garden of spices from which sweet odours arise. In Scripture, fruit speaks of the excellencies of Christ, but the spices, with their fragrance, speak of worship that has Christ for its object. In worship there is no thought of receiving blessing from Christ, but of bringing the homage of our hearts to Christ. When the wise men from the East found themselves in the presence of "the young Child", they fell down and "worshipped Him", and "presented unto Him gifts; gold, and frankincense and myrrh" (Matthew 2:11).When Mary anointed the feet of Jesus with "a pound of ointment of spikenard, very costly," she was not, as on other occasions, at His feet as a receiver to get instruction, or find sympathy in her sorrow; she was there as a *giver* to render the worship of a heart filled with the sense of His blessedness. It was good to be at His feet to hear His word, and, again, to be at His feet to receive comfort in sorrow, but in neither case do we read of the ointment with its odour. But when she is at His feet as a worshipper, with her precious ointment, we read, "the whole house was filled with the odour of the ointment" (John 12:1-3).

The Philippian saints, in their gift to the Apostle, may indeed have shown forth some of the excellencies of Christ — His comfort of love and compassions — and thus bring forth fruit that would abound to their account; but there was in their gift the spirit of sacrifice and worship which was as "an odour of a sweet smell, a sacrifice acceptable, well pleasing to God" (Philippians 2:1; 4:17-18).

In our day, if our hearts are to be a garden of the Lord, let us not forget that the Lord not only looks for the precious fruits of the Spirit, reproducing in us something of His lovely traits, but also the spirit of worship that rises up to Him as a sweet odour.

A REFRESHING GARDEN

Lastly, the Lord would have His garden to be a source of refreshment to the world around. A garden from whence there flow the "living waters". Thus the Lord can speak of the believer, indwelt by the Holy Spirit, as being a source of blessing to a needy world, as He says, "Out of his belly shall flow rivers of living water" (John 7:38-39).

Thus we learn, from the Song of Songs, that the Lord would fain possess our hearts as a garden of delights for

Himself. He stands at the door of our hearts and knocks, for He desires to come in and dwell within our hearts. If we are slow to let Him in, He may say, as the Bridegroom in the Song, "Awake, O north wind; and come thou south; blow upon my garden, that the spices thereof may flow out." He may allow adverse circumstances, trials, and sorrows, in order to drive us to Himself, so that we may say like the bride, "Let my Beloved come into His garden."

If we open to Him we shall experience the truth of His own words, "If any man hear My voice, and open the door, I will come in to him, and will sup with him, and he with Me" (Revelation 3:20). In like spirit, when the bride says, "Let my Beloved come into his garden," the Bridegroom at once responds, "I am come into my garden, my sister, my spouse: I have gathered my myrrh with my spice; I have eaten my honeycomb with my honey."

If then, the heart of the believer be kept separate from the world, preserved from evil, and set apart for the Lord it will become like "a garden enclosed."

In that garden there will be found a spring of secret joy and refreshment that, like a fountain, rises to its source.

The fountain, springing up to its source, will bring forth precious fruit, the excellencies of Christ.

The fruit that speaks of the moral traits of Christ in the heart of the believer, will lead to worship that rises up as a sweet odour to the heart of Christ.

The heart that goes out in worship to Christ will become a source of blessing to the world around.

In the light of these Scriptures we may well pray the prayer of the Apostle when he bows his knees to the

THE GARDEN OF THE LORD

Father, and asks, "That He would grant you, according to the riches of His glory, to be strengthened with might by His Spirit in the inner man; that *Christ may dwell in your hearts by faith*" (Ephesians 3:14-17).

> A wretched thing it were, to have our heart
> Like a thronged highway or a populous street,
> Where every idle thought has leave to meet,
> Pause, or pass on as in an open mart;
> Or like some road-side pool, which no nice art
> Has guarded that the cattle might not beat
> And foul it with a multitude of feet,
> Till of the heavens it can give back no part.
> But keep thou thine a holy solitude,
> For He, who would walk there, would walk alone;
> He who would drink there, must be first endued
> With single right to call that stream His own;
> Keep thou thine heart, close-fastened, unrevealed,
> A fencèd garden and a fountain sealed.[22]

---

[22] Richard Chevenix Trench, *Sonnet* in *The Story of Justin Martyr, and Other Poems*, Second Edition, London: Edward Moxon, 1836

"Abide in Me"

On that touching occasion when the Lord was alone with His disciples, communicating His farewell words of comfort, and imparting to them His last instructions, again and again He presses the deep necessity, as well as the blessedness, of abiding in Him. We hear Him say,

> "*Abide in Me*, and I in you. As the branch cannot bear fruit of itself, except it abide in the vine; no more can ye, except ye *abide in Me*. I am the vine, ye are the branches: He that *abideth in Me*, and I in him, the same bringeth forth much fruit: for without Me ye can do nothing... If ye *abide in Me*, and My words abide in you, ye shall ask what ye will, and it shall be done unto you."
>
> (John 15:4-7).

Again, the beloved Apostle, who heard these farewell words from the lips of the Lord, passes them on to believers in his Epistle. There we read:

> "He that saith he *abideth in Him* ought himself also so to walk, even as He walked."

> "And now, little children, *abide in Him*; that, when He shall appear, we may have boldness, and not be ashamed before Him at His coming."

"ABIDE IN ME"

"Whosoever *abideth in Him* sinneth not."

(1 John 2:6, 28; 3:6).

If, then, these verses set before us the blessedness of abiding in Christ, we may well pause to enquire, "What are we to understand by the Lord's words, 'Abide in Me'?" Do they not imply a walk in such *nearness to Christ* that the soul delights in all His loveliness and moral excellences, and thus finds in Him its object and perfect pattern?

Again, does not abiding in Christ suppose a heart in *communion with Christ*, that delights to confide in Him and learn of Him?

Above all, does not abiding in Christ imply a life lived under the *influence of His presence*, realised by faith? If a saintly and Christlike man of God visited our home, would not his presence have a restraining influence upon everyone in the home? We should probably be a little more careful than usual of our words and ways. If this would be the effect of the presence of a man of like passions with ourselves, what would be the effect of the realised presence of Christ, Himself? At times sad scenes have taken place, even among the Lord's people, in which we may have had our humbling part, when envy and strife prevailed, and believers have thoughtlessly, or even maliciously, wounded one another with bitter and offensive words. We may try to excuse our strong words. But should we not do well to ask ourselves, "What would have happened if the Lord had silently, but visibly, walked into our midst?" Should we not have to confess that under the influence of His presence many a bitter and offensive word would never have been uttered?

How good, then, it would be if we could ever remember that though the Lord is not visible to sight, yet He hears,

He sees, He knows. Well indeed does the Psalmist ask, "He that planted the ear, shall He not hear? He that formed the eye, shall He not see? ... He that teacheth man knowledge, shall not He know?" (Psalm 94:9-10).

To walk, then, in the consciousness that He listens to our words; that He sees our every act; that He reads our thoughts, is to walk under the blessed influence of His presence and thus *abide in Him*.

Furthermore, these Scriptures, that exhort us to abide in Christ, tell us also the blessedness we shall enjoy if we do abide in Him.

FRUIT-BEARING LIVES

First, we learn that abiding in Christ we shall bring forth fruit. The importance of this is pressed upon us by being stated both negatively and positively. We are told that unless we abide in Christ we cannot bring forth fruit. Then we are told that if we abide in Christ, and He in us, we shall bring forth much fruit. From another Scripture we learn that the fruit of the Spirit is "love, joy, peace, longsuffering, kindness, goodness, fidelity, meekness, self-control" (Galatians 5:22-23, N.Tr.). What are these lovely qualities but a description of the beautiful character of Christ? So we may surely say that the fruit of which the Lord speaks is the reproduction of His own character in the lives of believers.

The fruit, in this passage, is not service or the exercise of gift, however important in its place. Of necessity gifts are confined to the few: but it is open to all, young and old alike, to express something of the loveliness of Christ in their lives. Any little setting forth of the graces of Christ goes up as fruit to the Father, and goes out as testimony to the world. This, then, is the great object for which we are left in this dark world, to shine as lights by exhibiting something of the beautiful character of Christ. This will only be possible as we abide in Christ. We shall never exhibit the character of Christ by simply trying to be like Christ. If, however, we seek His Company, and come under His influence, by abiding in Him, we shall be changed into His image from glory to glory.

> Yet sure, if in Thy presence
> My soul still constant were,
> Mine eye would, more familiar,
> Its brighter glories bear.
>
> And thus, thy deep perfections
> Much better should I know,
> And with adoring fervour
> In this Thy nature grow.[23]

ANSWERED PRAYERS

Secondly, the Lord's words plainly tell us that, abiding in Christ, our prayers will have an answer. If under the blessed influence of His presence, with His words abiding in our hearts, our thoughts would be formed by His thoughts and our prayers would be in accord with His mind. Thus praying, we should have an answer to our prayers.

CHRIST-LIKE WALK

Thirdly, the Apostle John tells us, in his Epistle, that abiding in Him will lead to a "walk, even as He walked" (1 John 2:6). How did Christ walk? Of Him we read, "Christ pleased not Himself" {Romans 15:3}. Speaking of the Father, the Lord Himself could say, "I do always those things that please Him" {John 8:29}. This is the perfect pattern for the believer's walk for the Apostle Paul can say, we "ought to walk and please God" (1 Thessalonians 4:1, N.Tr.). Again, the same Apostle exhorts believers to "walk in love, as Christ also hath loved us" (Ephesians 5:2).

---

[23] J. N. Darby, 1845

Thus, may we not say, the outstanding marks of the Lord's path were the entire absence of self-will in doing the Father's will, and the serving of others in love. For us, it is only possible in any measure to tread such a path of perfection as we abide in Christ. How good, then, like Mary of old to sit at His feet and hear His words. Thus under His influence to recall His path, to trace His footsteps, to listen to His words of love and grace, to see His hand stretched forth to bless, and, behind all His perfect walk and ways and words, to discern the spirit of One who ever set aside all thoughts of self, in order to serve others in love.

We may know the doctrines of Christianity; we may rightly hold the great essential truths of our faith, but, as one has said, "no amount of knowledge however correct, no amount of intelligence, however exact, will ever put upon your soul the impress of the mind of the Lord Jesus Christ."[24] If we are to wear the impress of Christ — if, as we pass along we are to have some sense of Him, we must be in His company, and walk with Him. Every man is formed by the company that he keeps: the character of the one in whose company we walk, is the character we shall reflect. We must abide in Christ and thus walk with Christ, if we are to be like Christ and walk as He walked.

Consistent ways

Fourthly, the Apostle John further tells us that if abiding in Christ our walk will be such that we shall not be ashamed before Christ at His coming. Oftentimes there is much in our walk, and ways, and speech, and manners, that passes current with men, and even among the people of God, and of which we may judge very lightly when viewed by human standards. If, however, we were to judge

---

[24] Walter Thomas Turpin, *The Man Christ Jesus: Addresses on the Gospel of Luke*, London: W H Broom & Rouse, 1880

ourselves, and our words, and ways, in the light of the coming glory of the appearing of Christ, should we not find much that we should have to condemn, and confess with shame, as far short of the standard of glory?

Only as we abide in Christ, under the influence of His presence, and so walk in self-judgment, shall we be preserved from all that which would cause shame in the day of glory.

Preserved from lawlessness

Fifthly, we are reminded by the Apostle John, that "Whosoever abideth in Him sinneth not" (1 John 3:6). From the preceding verses we learn what the Spirit of God means by sin, for we read, in verse 4, "sin is lawlessness" (N.Tr.). The essence of sin is doing one's own will without reference to God or man. The world around is increasingly marked by lawlessness — everyone doing that which is right in his own eyes. The result being that, in spite of civilisation, education, and legislation, the world system is breaking up, and society and nations are increasingly disintegrating. Wherever the spirit of lawlessness prevails, disintegration will follow, whether it be in the world or among the people of God. As believers we are ever in danger of being affected by the spirit of the world around. Thus it has come to pass that through lack of watchfulness the same principle of lawlessness, that is breaking up the world system, has wrought division and scattering among the people of God.

If, in a school, each pupil was allowed to do his own will the school would inevitably break up. If each member of a family followed his own will the family would be wrecked; and if each individual of a company of believers pursues his own will, disruption must follow. The spirit of lawlessness, in whatever sphere it shows itself, will lead to disintegration, and the greater the sincerity of those who pursue their own will, the greater the harm they will cause. There is no greater cause of disruption among the people of God than the determined self-will of a sincere man.

How then are we to escape the evil principle of lawlessness, or self-will? Only by abiding in Christ; for the Apostle says, 'Whosoever abideth in Him sinneth not" {1 John 3:6}. Only as we are held under the influence of the One who could say, "I came ... not to do mine own will, but the will of Him that sent Me" {John 6:38}, shall we escape the self-will that is the very essence of sin.

These, then, are the blessed results, as brought before us in Scripture, of abiding in Christ. If answering to the Lord's words by seeking to abide in Him:

- Our lives would bear fruit by expressing something of the lovely character of Christ.
- Our prayers, being according to His mind, would have an answer.
- Our path would show forth something of the beauty of His walk.
- Our ways would be consistent with the coming glory of Christ.
- Our walk would be preserved from the lawlessness of the flesh that has its origin in the devil, that is the root cause of the ruin of man and the sorrows of the world.

How good, then, to heed the Lord's word, "Abide in Me ... for without Me ye can do nothing." We may be gifted and have all knowledge, and zeal, we may have long experience, but it still remains true that without Christ we can do nothing. Gift, and knowledge, and zeal, are not power. All these things will not enable us to overcome the

"ABIDE IN ME"

flesh, to refuse the world, or escape the snares of the devil. We may have all these things yet *without Christ*, we may stumble at the smallest trial and fall into the greatest evils.

If, then, "without Christ" we can do nothing, let us seek to abide in Him and not dare to go forward for one day, or take a single step, without Him.

> Oh keep my soul, then, Jesus,
>   Abiding still with Thee,
> And if I wander, teach me
>   Soon back to Thee to flee.[25]

---

[25] J. N. Darby, 1845

Epistles of Christ

READ 2 CORINTHIANS 3

In the Third Chapter of the Second Epistle to the Corinthians the Apostle Paul brings Christ before our souls in three ways.

- First, Christ is presented as written upon the hearts of the believers that formed the Assembly at Corinth (verse 3).
- Secondly, Christ is presented as manifested to "all men" by this Assembly (verses 2-3).
- Thirdly, Christ is presented as a living Person in the glory — the Object before these believers (verse 18).

Thus there passes before us God's intention that, during the absence of Christ from this world, there should be gatherings of believers on earth who have Christ written upon their hearts; Christ manifested in their lives; and Christ before them as an Object in the glory.

As we read the last touching instructions of the Lord to His disciples, and as we reverently listen to the Lord's prayer to the Father, we are made conscious that underlying both the discourses and the prayer, there is ever kept before us the great truth that believers are left in this world to represent Christ — the Man that has gone to glory. It is God's intention that though Christ personally is no longer here, yet Christ morally should still be seen in His people. Further, it is manifest that all the Epistles press upon us our privilege, and our responsibility, as believers, to represent the character of Christ to a world that has rejected and cast Him out.

In the addresses to the Seven Churches in Revelation, we are permitted to view the Lord walking in the midst of the Churches taking account of their condition, and giving us His judgment as to how far they have answered to, or failed in, their responsibility. In result we learn that the great mass of those who profess His Name, have not only entirely failed to represent His character before the world, but have become so hopelessly corrupt and indifferent to Himself that in the end, they will be spued out of His mouth and thus utterly rejected. Nevertheless, we also learn that in the midst of this vast profession there will be, until the end of the Church's history on earth, some who, though they have but a little strength, will answer to His mind by setting forth something of the loveliness of His character.

Seeing, then, that it is still possible, even in a day of ruin, to express something of the character of Christ, surely everyone who loves the Lord will say, "I would like to answer to the Lord's mind and be of the number who, in some little measure, manifest something of the beautiful traits of Christ to the world around."

It is true that it is possible for the world to form some estimate of Christ from the Word of God; but, apart from the Word — which they may call in question, or fail to understand, even if read — it is God's intention that in the lives of His people there should be a presentation of Christ "known and read of all men" {verse 2}.

This being so, it becomes a searching question for us all, "if the men of this world are to gain their impression of Christ from the gatherings of His people, what conclusion will they reach as to Christ, as they look upon our individual lives; as well as the collective life of God's people?" Let us remember the Lord's searching words, "By this shall all men know that ye are My disciples, if ye have love one to another" {John 13:35}. Apply such a test to the gathering with which we may be connected, and should we not have to hang our heads with shame as we recall occasions when envy, evil speaking, and backbiting, were more in evidence than the meekness and gentleness of Christ. Let us remember that whatever the circumstances — even if called to face reproaches and insults — our one business should be to set forth the character of Christ. One has said, "It is better to lose your coat, than to let go the character of Christ."

If, then, we would answer to the Lord's mind and set forth His character before the world, we shall do well to heed the teaching of the Apostle in this portion of the Word.

CHRIST WRITTEN ON THE HEART

First, then, let us notice that the Apostle speaks of these believers as "the epistle of Christ" {verse 3}. He does not say the "epistles" but the "epistle", for he is not thinking simply of what is true of individuals, but of the whole company, though, obviously, the company is composed of individuals.

Then let us remark, that the Apostle does not say "Ye should be the epistle of Christ", but that "Ye are the epistle of Christ". Entertaining the wrong thought that we ought to be epistles of Christ, we shall set to work to become such by our own efforts. This would not only lead us into legal occupation with ourselves, but would also shut out the work of "the Spirit of the living God" {verse 3}. The fact is that we become epistles of Christ, not by our own efforts but by the Spirit of God writing Christ upon our hearts.

A Christian is one to whom Christ has become precious by a work of the Spirit in the heart. It is not simply a knowledge of Christ in the head, which an unconverted man may have, that constitutes a man a Christian, but Christ written in the heart. As sinners we discover our need of Christ, and are burdened with our sins. We find relief by discovering that Christ by His propitiatory work has died for our sins, and that God has set forth His acceptance of that work by seating Christ in the glory. We rest in God's satisfaction with Christ and His work, and our affections are drawn out to the One through whom we have been blessed. "Unto you therefore which believe He is precious" {1 Peter 2:7}. Thus Christ is written on our hearts and we become the epistle of Christ. If we are not the epistle of Christ we are not Christians at all.

CHRIST MANIFESTED TO ALL MEN

Having set forth the true Christian company as composed of believers upon whose hearts Christ has been written, the Apostle presents the second great truth when he says, not only, "Ye are the epistle of Christ", but also, *"Ye are manifestly declared to be the epistle of Christ"* {verse 3}, *"known and read of all men"* {verse 2}.

It is one thing for a gathering of believers to be an epistle of Christ, and quite another for the gathering to be in such a right condition that they manifest to all men something of the character of Christ. The responsibility of any gathering of saints is, not to walk well in order to become an epistle, but, seeing they are an epistle of

Christ, to walk well in order that the epistle may be read of all men. If anyone writes a letter of commendation it is to commend the person named in the letter. So when the Spirit of God writes Christ on the hearts of believers, it is in order that they together may become an epistle of commendation to commend Christ to the world around. That by their holy and separate walk, their mutual love to one another, their lowliness and meekness, their gentleness and grace, they may set forth the lovely character of Christ.

Thus it was with the Corinthian saints. They had, indeed, been walking in a disorderly way: but, as the result of the Apostle's first letter, they had cleared themselves from evil so that the Apostle can now say, not only that as an Assembly they were an epistle of Christ, but, that they were an epistle "known and read of all men".

Alas! the writing may become indistinct, but it does not cease to be a letter because it is blotted and blurred. Christians are often like the writing on some ancient tomb stone. There are faint indications of an inscription, a capital letter, here and there, would indicate some name was once written on the stone. But it is so weatherworn, and dirt-begrimed, that it is hardly possible to decipher the writing. So, alas, may it be with ourselves. When first the Spirit writes Christ upon the hearts of a company of saints, their affections are warm and their collective life speaks plainly of Christ. The writing, being fresh and clear, is known and read of all men. But, as time passes, unless there is watchfulness, and self-judgment, envying, strife, and bitterness, may creep in, and the gathering cease to give any true impression of Christ.

Nevertheless, in spite of all our failure, Christians are the epistle of Christ and it ever remains true that it is God's great intention that all men should see the character of

Christ set forth in His people. Here, then, we have a beautiful description of the true Christian company. It is a company of individual believers, gathered to Christ, upon whose hearts Christ has been written, not with ink, but "with the Spirit of the living God; not in tables of stone, but in fleshly tables of the heart" {verse 3}. As in the tables of stone of old, men could read what the righteousness of God demanded from man under law, so, now, in the lives of God's people, the world should read what the love of God brings to man under grace.

Christ The Object in Glory

How then, we may ask, is the writing of Christ on the hearts of God's people to be kept clear and legible, so that, in the gathering of God's people the character of Christ can be manifest to all men?

The answer to this question brings us to the third great truth of the chapter. Christ will be manifested to all men only as we have before us the living Christ in the glory as our Object. So the Apostle writes, "We all looking on the glory of the Lord with unveiled face, are transformed according to the same image from glory to glory" (verse 18, N.Tr.). There is a transforming power in beholding the Lord in glory. This transforming power is available for all believers — the youngest as well as the oldest; *"we all,"* not simply "we Apostles", beholding the glory of the Lord "are changed into the same image". This change is not affected by our own efforts, nor by wearying ourselves in the endeavour to be like the Lord. Nor is it by seeking to imitate some devoted saint. It is by beholding the glory of the Lord. There is no veil on His face, and as we behold Him, not only will every veil of darkness pass from our hearts, but morally we shall become increasingly like Him, changing from glory to glory. Gazing upon the Lord in glory we are lifted above all the weakness and failure that we find in ourselves, and all the evil around, to discover and delight in His perfection. As the bride in the Song of Songs can say, "I sat down under His shadow with great delight, and His fruit was sweet to my taste" {Song of Songs 2:3}.

In the course of the Epistle the Apostle gives us a taste of some of this precious fruit. Turning to 2 Corinthians 5:14, we read that *"the love of Christ* constraineth us." Here the love of Christ is presented as the true motive for all ministry, whether to saints or sinners. The greatest expression of that love was His death. "Greater love hath no man than this, that a man lay down his life for his friends" {John 15:13}. Again we read, "Christ also loved the Church, and gave Himself for it" {Ephesians 5:25}. With such love before his soul the Apostle can well say, "that they which live should not henceforth live unto themselves, but unto Him which died for them, and rose again" {2 Corinthians 5:15}. In the light of this Scripture we may well challenge our hearts as to the motive that actuates us in all our service. Is it the love of Christ that constrains us, or is it the love of self? Are we living unto ourselves, or are we living "unto Him", and thus, like Him, willing to forget self in order to serve others in love? One has said, "Alas! how often have we to reproach ourselves with going on in a round of Christian duty, faithful in general intention, but not flowing from the fresh realisation of the love of Christ to our soul."[26]

Passing to 2 Corinthians 8:9, we come to another lovely characteristic of Christ. There we read of *"the grace of our Lord Jesus Christ"*. The Apostle is pleading on behalf of the poor Jewish believers, urging the richer Corinthian saints to help in meeting their necessities. In both verses 6 and

---

[26] J. N. Darby, *Collected Writings*, Volume 5, Seven Lectures on the Prophetical Addresses to the Seven Churches, Lecture 2, 1852

7, he speaks of giving as a "grace". Then he sets before us Christ as the One in whom we have a transcendent example of the grace of giving. He was rich, surpassingly rich, and yet to meet our deep needs He not only gives, but, such is His grace that, *He becomes poor to give*. "For your sakes He became poor, that ye through His poverty might be rich" {verse 9}. By the incarnation He became poor, and His poverty is witnessed by the manger at Bethlehem and the humble home at Nazareth, and that, in the days of His ministry He Himself said, the "Foxes have holes, and birds of the air have nests; but the Son of Man hath not where to lay His head" (Luke 9:58). To reach a poor fallen woman and bring heaven's best gifts to earth's worst sinners, He became a poor, needy, and lonely man by a well side. The very moment when He is enriching us with a fountain of water springing up unto eternal life He Himself has become so poor that he has to ask for a drink of water (John 4:7, 14).

Turning to 2 Corinthians 10:1, we find some more refreshing fruit that marked the life of Christ. First we read of *"the meekness of Christ"*. The Apostle is correcting the spirit of rivalry that had been working amongst the Corinthian saints, whereby some of the gifted servants were measuring themselves with one another, and seeking to commend themselves. So doing they were walking in the flesh, and warring after the flesh, glorying in their gifts, talking about themselves, boasting in their work, and belittling the Apostle. To correct their vanity and self-assertiveness, he brings before them the meekness of Christ who never asserted His rights, or defended Himself; "who, when He was reviled, reviled not again" {1 Peter 2:23}. The chief priests may defame Him, but "Jesus held His peace"; He is falsely accused before Pilate, but "He answered him to never a word"; He is mocked by Herod, but "He answered him nothing" {Matthew 26:63,

27:14; Luke 23:9}. Good for us, if, in the presence of defamation and insults we could catch something of the spirit of the Lord and show the meekness that refuses to assert our rights, stand upon our dignity, or defend ourselves.

Then the Apostle speaks of *"the gentleness of Christ"*. Another lovely quality that He ever exhibited in the presence of opposition. Seeking to obey the word of the Lord and maintain the truth we shall soon find that there are those who will oppose and raise questions that lead to strife. But "the servant of the Lord must not strive" but seek to act in the spirit of the Lord and be "*gentle* unto all men, apt to teach, patient" {2 Timothy 2:24}. The gentleness of Christ speaks of the manner in which He acted and spoke. How often, with ourselves, even if our motive is right, and the principles we stand for are true, all is spoilt because our manner is lacking in graciousness and gentleness. Let us remember the striking words of the Psalmist, "Thy gentleness hath made me great" (Psalm 18:35). Our vehemence may easily degenerate into violence by which we belittle ourselves in the eyes of others; but gentleness will make us great. Violence draws out violence; but gentleness is irresistible.[27] "The fruit of the Spirit is… gentleness" {Galatians 5:22}.

Finally, in 2 Corinthians 12:9, we read of *"the power of Christ"*. The Apostle is speaking of bodily infirmities, insults, necessities, persecutions, and distresses. He learned by experience that all these things only become an occasion for the manifestation of "the power of Christ" to preserve the believer through the trials and lift him above them. Thus we learn that whatever the trial, His "grace is sufficient", and His "strength is made perfect in weakness".

---

[27] H. Martyn, 1806

Thus, with our eyes upon Christ in the glory, we are reminded by the Apostle of the perfections of Christ as He passes before us:

- "The love of Christ",
- "The grace of our Lord Jesus Christ",
- "The meekness of Christ",
- "The gentleness of Christ", and
- "The power of Christ".

As we look at Christ in the glory and admire these lovely moral traits, set forth in all their perfection in Christ, we find His fruit sweet to our taste, and, almost unconsciously to ourselves, shall begin to exhibit something of His gracious character, and thus become changed into His image.

Thus the Holy Spirit not only writes Christ on the heart so that we become epistles of Christ, but, by engaging our hearts with Christ in glory, He transforms us into His image and so keeps the writing clear that it may be read of all men.

What a wonderful testimony it would be if the world could look upon any little company of the Lord's people and see in them "love", and "grace", and "meekness", and "gentleness", and a "power" that enables them to rise above all circumstances.

May we realise, in deeper measure, that it is the mind of God that His people should be the epistle of Christ to manifest Christ to all men, by having Christ in the glory before us as our one Object.

In His Steps

"Follow His steps: who did no sin, neither was guile found in His mouth: Who, when He was reviled, reviled not again; when He suffered, He threatened not; but committed Himself to Him that judgeth righteously."

(1 Peter 2:21-23).

"Take My yoke upon you, and learn of Me; for I am meek and lowly in heart: and ye shall find rest unto your souls. For My yoke is easy, and My burden is light."

(Matthew 11:29-30).

While the Lord Jesus Christ is the great theme of all Scripture, yet every several portion presents some special aspect of His Person or work. The above passages bring before us, very blessedly, the lowly grace that marked His pathway of suffering as the perfectly subject Man.

In one passage we are exhorted by the Apostle Peter to follow His steps: in the other, believers are invited by the Lord, Himself, to learn of Him. Good for each one to heed the exhortation and to respond to the gracious invitation. To do so however, we need to reverently enquire: "What are His steps that we are exhorted to follow?" and, "What is it that the Lord would have us to learn of Him?"

"His Steps"
Read 1 Peter 2:21-23

First, let us listen to the exhortation of the Apostle. There came a day in the history of Peter when the Lord had said to His restored disciple, "Follow Me" (John 21:19). Now the Apostle passes on these words to each one of us, as he says, "Follow His steps." In Christendom, and even by true believers, the words "Follow His steps" are often used in a vague and loose way. Even unconverted people will seize upon these words, misusing them to convey the false thought that if men carry out the precepts of the Sermon on the Mount they will be very good Christians, and thereby secure the salvation of their souls. Probably those who speak thus lightly about following His steps, would be at a loss to turn to the Scripture where the exhortation is found, and even so would prefer their own interpretation of the words rather than enquire as to the meaning with which they are used by the Holy Spirit.

Turning to the passage in which the exhortation occurs, we at once learn from the context that these words are addressed to believers — those of whom the Apostle can say that they have received the end of their faith even the salvation of their souls (1 Peter 1:9). It is evident then that in this Scripture there is no exhortation to a sinner to follow His steps in order to obtain salvation. Apart from the sacrificial death of Christ, and faith in His precious blood, there can be no salvation for a helpless sinner. In Scripture God never uses *"His steps"* to set aside *His work*.

The exhortation to "follow His steps" is then addressed to believers, and moreover, is used with a very distinct meaning. What this meaning is we learn from the four distinct steps that are set before us. It is evident that a great deal that the Lord did in His marvellous life we cannot, and are not asked to, do. He did mighty works, even to raising the dead; He spake as never man spake. In these ways we are not exhorted to follow His steps. The four steps we are exhorted to follow are possible for all believers, from the youngest to the oldest.

First, we are reminded that He "did no sin." We know that He went about doing good; and, in this same Epistle we are exhorted, again and again, to "good works," and to "do well" {2:12, 14, 20; 3:6}. Here, however, the exhortation takes a negative form; we are to follow His steps in this respect, that He did no sin. Whatever happens, whatever circumstances may arise, whatever rebuffs we may have to meet, whatever wrongs we may have to suffer, whatever insults we may have to endure, *we are to do no sin.* It is comparatively easy to do good as a benefactor, meeting the needs of others; but, seeing we have the flesh in us, it is at times difficult to do no sin. It is a greater thing to do no sin in trying circumstances than to do good in easy ones. The Lord was perfect in all circumstances, and, whatever the circumstances we have to meet, our first care should be to follow His steps, and maintain His character, in this respect, that we do no sin. It is better to suffer wrong than sin; better to lose your coat than let go the character of Christ.

Secondly, we read, "neither was guile found in His mouth." However sorely tried by wicked men, no question that He asked, no answer that He gave, no word that fell from His lips, was ever marred by any trace of guile. Alas! with us, at times, malice and envy may lurk behind words that are "smoother than butter" and "softer than oil" {Psalm 55:21}. With Him no evil motive was ever hidden under fair speech. Guile lurked behind the apparently innocent question of the religious Pharisees when they asked "Is it lawful to give tribute unto Caesar, or not?" for we read they were seeking to "entangle Him in His talk" (Matthew 22:15-18). With the flesh in us it is all too possible to seek to entangle one another with smooth speech and innocent looking questions. Alas! we can even covertly attack one another in the very words we address to God in public prayer. How good then, and necessary the exhortation to follow in the steps of the One in whose mouth no guile was found.

Thirdly, we are reminded that the Lord was One, "Who when He was reviled, reviled not again; when He suffered, He threatened not." In the presence of insults, false accusation, and malicious charges, He remained silent. When falsely accused before the Jewish Council, He "held His peace." To the accusations of the Jews, in the presence of Pilate, "He answered nothing." To Pilate, himself, "He answered... never a word." The mocking Herod may question Him in many words, "but He answered him nothing" (Matthew 26:63; 27:12, 14; Luke 23:9). How good for us to follow in His steps and, in the presence of the malicious words of men, come from what quarter they may, to keep silence. From other Scriptures it is clear that the Christian may "entreat," "exhort," and even "rebuke," but never is he to revile or threaten.

Fourthly, He "committed Himself to Him that judgeth righteously." To do no sin, to speak no guile, to keep silence in the presence of malicious words, have a negative character. This last step is positive. If we keep silence in the presence of insults, it is not that there is no answer to evil and malice, but rather that the answer is left with God. We are never to attempt to take vengeance upon the wrongdoer. God retains all vengeance in His own hands. He has said, "*Vengeance belongeth unto Me*, I will recompense, saith the Lord. And again, The Lord shall judge His people" (Hebrews 10:30). Our part then is to follow in the steps of the Lord Jesus, and in the presence of insults to commit ourselves unto Him that judgeth righteously, remembering that word which says, "Avenge not yourselves, but rather give place unto wrath: for it is written, Vengeance is mine: I will repay saith the Lord" (Romans 12:19). Again we may recall the words of the prophet, "Jehovah is good unto them that wait for Him, to the soul [that] seeketh Him. It is good that one should both wait, *and that in silence*, for the salvation of Jehovah" (Lamentations 3:24-26, N.Tr.).

Here, then, we have four steps, taken in perfection by the Lord, that we are exhorted to follow. In all these steps there is no word as to ministry, or any form of service, that would make any show in this world, or bring us into prominence amongst the people of God. This being so we might thoughtlessly say, as we read these exhortations, that to do no evil, speak no guile, to keep silence in the presence of insults, and commit oneself to God, does not seem after all very much, and is a little disappointing. If, however, we put these things into practice, and follow His steps it will assuredly be found that our brethren *will not be disappointed in us*. Could we but take these steps others would see in us the most wonderful sight that can be seen in this world — they would see A CHRIST-LIKE MAN.

God forbid that we should belittle true service for Christ, but let us not forget that we may travel worldwide in service, and preach to thousands, and our names be well known in religious circles, and our service duly recorded in religious papers, and yet all be of little account in God's sight, if these four steps are lacking. Let us remember that we may speak with the tongues of angels and yet be nothing. So that, in the day to come it is possible that a thousand of our fine sermons, on which perhaps we prided ourselves, and for which our brethren may have praised us, will be found to be but dust and ashes, while some little bit of Christ in our lives, which we may have entirely forgotten, will shine out in all its beauty and receive its bright reward. Thus these steps may not take us into the public gaze today, but they will take us far into the Kingdom glories in the day to come. It is a word we do well to remember, "Many that are first shall be last; and the last first" (Mark 10:31).

"Learn of Me"
Read Matthew 11:29-30

It will greatly help us to carry out the Apostle's exhortation to "follow His steps" if we heed the Lord's own words, "Learn of Me." To learn of the Lord, we must "*Consider Him* that endured such contradiction of sinners" {Hebrews 12:3}.

In the early chapters of the Gospel of Matthew we see the Lord in the midst of Israel, on every hand dispensing grace and power in relieving men of every pressure under which they are found. He healed the sick, fed the hungry, clothed the naked, delivered from the power of Satan, forgave sins, and raised the dead. In result men fought against Him without a cause, rewarded Him evil for good and hatred for love (Psalm 109:5). They laughed him to scorn; they said, "He casteth out devils through the prince of the devils," and that He was "a man gluttonous, and a winebibber" (Matthew 9:24, 34; 11:19).

In the presence of the contradiction of sinners, of the hatred that spurned His love, and the evil that scorned His goodness, how did He act? In the presence of all this enmity we read, that He gave Himself unto prayer (Psalm 109:4). Instead of turning upon His opposers and reviling those that reviled Him, He turned to God in prayer and committed Himself to Him that judgeth righteously.

"THE LORD IS MY SHEPHERD"

> In scorn, neglect, reviling,
>   Thy patient grace stood firm:
> Man's malice unavailing
>   To move Thy heart to haste.[28]

Thus in this wonderful scene described in Matthew 11, which sums up the effect of His mighty works in the midst of Israel, we are permitted to see how the Lord acts when He is despised and rejected of men. We see Him turning to the Father in prayer, and we hear Him say, "even so, Father: for so it seemed good in Thy sight" {Matthew 11:26}. He submits entirely to the Father's will and takes everything from His hand. Then, with Himself before us as the perfect Example, we hear Him say to us,

"Take my yoke upon you, and learn of Me."

In Scripture the "yoke" is ever a figure of submission to the will of another. From the beginning to the end of His wonderful path through this world, the Lord, as the perfect Man, was here for the will of the Father. Coming into the world, He could say, "Lo, I come to do thy will, O God." Passing through the world he could say, "I came down from heaven, not to do Mine own will, but the will of Him that sent Me", and again, He says, "I do always those things that please Him." Going out of the world, He could say, in view of the cross, "Not My will, but Thine, be done" (Hebrews 10:9, John 6:38; 8:29; Luke 22:42).

Our little circumstances, however painful and trying at times, are as nothing compared with those the Lord had to face. But whatever they may be we are exhorted to take the Lord's yoke by quietly submitting to what the Father allows.

Moreover, the Lord says, "Learn of Me: for I am meek and lowly in heart." He was not only meek and lowly in

---
[28] J. N. Darby, 1867

manner, but He was "meek and lowly *in heart*." The right manner that men can see is comparatively easy to put on, but the right condition of heart, that the Lord alone can see, can only result from turning to the Lord in prayer and submitting to the Father's will. Naturally we are neither meek nor lowly. Instead of meekly giving way to others we assert ourselves; instead of having low thoughts of self we are naturally prone to self-importance. To correct all these natural tendencies of the flesh the Lord engages us with Himself, as He says, "Learn of Me." As we gaze upon Him, and admire these lovely qualities, we insensibly become changed into His image. We become morally like the One we admire. Alas! the fact that oftentimes we are so little like Him tells, only too plainly, how little we have Himself before our souls — how little we learn of Him.

Taking His yoke and learning of Him we shall find rest unto our souls. Dwelling upon the trying circumstances we may have to meet, fretting our souls over the insults that may be flung at us, the betrayal of false friends, the malice of jealous persons, will bring no rest to the soul. Submitting to what the Father allows and catching the beautiful spirit of Christ, in all its meekness and lowliness, as we learn of Him, we shall enjoy the rest of spirit that was ever the portion of the Lord in a world of unrest.

Moreover, if we take His yoke, and thus submit to the Father's will, we shall find that His yoke is easy and His burden light. For in following His steps, doing no sin, speaking without guile, keeping silence in the presence of insults, and committing ourselves to God, we shall have His support as yoked with Him in submission to the Father's will. And with *His support*, and in fellowship with Him, we shall find how true are His words,

"*My yoke is easy, and My burden is light.*"

"THE LORD IS MY SHEPHERD"

Thus, as we read these Scriptures, we are made conscious that Peter does not exhort us to take impossible steps; and the Lord does not ask us to learn impossible lessons.

Peter exhorts us,

- To do no sin,
- To use no guile,
- To be silent in the presence of insults, and
- To commit ourselves to GOD.

The Lord asks us to learn of Him, in subjection to the Father's will, in meekness that thinks of others, and lowliness that does not think of self.

> We wonder at Thy lowly mind,
> And fain would like Thee be,
> And all our rest and pleasure find
> In learning, Lord, of Thee.[29]

---

[29] J. G. Deck, 1838

At His Feet

Of all the disciples of Christ that pass before us in the Gospel story, perhaps none are more marked by single-hearted devotedness to Christ than Mary of Bethany. She makes nothing of self, but everything of Christ, and hence, on the three occasions that she comes before us, she is found at the feet of Jesus.

We see her first in her sister's home at Bethany, when the Lord of life entered that home and Mary sat at His feet as a *learner* (Luke 10). Later, when death had entered the home, she is found at His feet as a *mourner* (John 11). Lastly, when a few of His loved ones make a supper for the Lord, who had just manifested His resurrection power and glory, she is found at His feet as a *worshipper*.

She not only knew that the Lord was the great Teacher come from God, the One who can sympathise with us in our sorrows, and the Object of our worship, but she had experienced His teaching, tasted His sympathy, and worshipped at His feet.

Good for us if, like the Apostle Paul, we can each say that the desire of the heart is "That I may know Him" {Philippians 3:10}. We may know much about Christ, but, in order to know Him we must be in His company and, at His feet, learn His mind through His word, taste His sympathy, and in His presence worship and adore.

It is true that the Lord delights to honour the one that puts honour upon Him in the day of His rejection, and has said that wheresoever the gospel is preached the story of Mary shall be told for a memorial of her. But the story of Mary has also been recorded for our profit, for all Scripture is given by God for our instruction. May we then, as we read her story, profit by her lowly and devoted life.

AT HIS FEET AS A LEARNER
READ LUKE 10:38-42

If, as sinners, we have been at the feet of the Saviour discovering that, in spite of all our sins, He loves us and has died for us, then, if we are to make spiritual progress — if we are to be "meet for the Master's use, and prepared unto every good work" — the "one thing needful," as believers, is to take our place at His feet and hear His word {2 Timothy 2:21, N.Tr.}.

This plain but important truth is brought before us in the homely scene described in the five closing verses of the tenth chapter of the Gospel of Luke. Journeying on His way to Jerusalem, we are told that the Lord came to a certain village, and a certain woman named Martha received Him into her house. She gladly opened her home to the Lord, and at once set herself to minister to His bodily needs. This indeed was right and beautiful in its place; and yet the story clearly shows that there was much of self in Martha's service. She did not like to have all the burden of this service, and felt grieved that she was left to serve alone. There was one thing lacking in her service.

The one thing needful — the one thing that Martha missed — was to sit at the feet of Jesus and hear His word.

AT HIS FEET

She loved the Lord, and with all her energy she zealously set herself to serve the Lord; but her zeal was not according to knowledge. She set herself to work without having first been in the company of the Lord, and in communion with the Lord, and therefore without being instructed in the mind of the Lord through the word of the Lord. As a result she was "distracted with much serving," was "careful and troubled about many things," complaining about her sister, and even entertaining the thought that the Lord was indifferent to her labours.

Alas! do we not, at times, act like Martha? We may take up service according to our own thoughts, or under the direction of others. From morning to night we may busy ourselves in a continual round of activity, and yet neglect the one thing needful — to be alone with the Lord, and in communion with Him hear His word and learn His mind. Little wonder that we get "distracted," and "troubled about many things," and complain of others. How true it is that it is easier to spend whole days in a round of busy service, than half an hour alone with Jesus.

In Mary we see a believer who chose the "good part." Sometimes it is said that Mary chose the better part, as if Martha's part was good, but Mary's was better. It is not thus that the Lord speaks. He definitely says that Mary's part was "that good part," for she chose the "one thing needful" — to sit at His feet and hear His word.

Clearly, then, Mary had a keener perception of the desires of the heart of Christ than her sister. One has said, "Martha's eye saw His weariness, and would give to Him: Mary's faith apprehended His fulness, and would draw from Him."[30]

---

[30] John Gifford Bellett, *Christian Friend*, Volume 14, 1887

Martha thought of the Lord only as One who was requiring something from us; Mary discerned that, beyond all the service of which He is so worthy, the desire of His heart, and the great purpose of His coming into this world, was to communicate something to us, "Grace and truth came by Jesus Christ," and, at the end of His path He could say, "I have given unto them the words which Thou gavest Me" (John 1:17; 17:8). By the word of God salvation is brought to us (Acts 13:26); by the word of God we are born again (1 Peter 1:23); by the word of God we are cleansed from defilement (John 15:3); by the word of God we are sanctified (John 17:17); and by the word of God we are instructed in all the truth of God "that the man of God may be perfect, thoroughly furnished unto all good works" (2 Timothy 3:15-17).

May we not say that Martha set herself to do good works without having been thoroughly furnished by the word of God? In Mary we learn that communion with Christ, and instruction in the word of Christ must precede all service that is acceptable to Christ. He delights that, in His own time and way, we should minister to Him; but, above all, He delights to have us in His company that He may minister to us.

Mary chose this good part and the Lord will not allow any complaints by her sister to belittle her choice — it shall not be taken from her. So, again, in the last days of the Church's history on earth, the Lord commends the Philadelphians, not for any great activity that would give them a prominent place before the world, but that they had "kept [His] word" {Revelation 3:8}. Like Mary of old they set greater store on His word than their works. It is not, indeed, that Mary was without works, for having chosen "that good part," in due time the Lord commends her for doing "a good work" (Matthew 26:10). So with the Philadelphian saints, the Lord who commended them for keeping His word, is the One who can say "I know thy works" {Revelation 3:8}.

Of old Moses could say of the LORD, "Yea, He loved the people; all His saints are in Thy hand: and they sat down at Thy feet; every one shall receive of Thy words" (Deuteronomy 33:3). This presents a lovely picture of the true position of God's people — held in the hand of the Lord; sitting at the feet of the Lord, and listening to the words of the Lord. Secure in His hand; at rest at His feet; and learning His mind. May we, then, choose this good part, and in due course do the good work.

AT HIS FEET AS A MOURNER
READ JOHN 11:32

In the touching scene described in the eleventh chapter of John, we again hear of the two sisters, Martha and Mary. Sickness had ended in death casting its shadow over the home. Their brother has been taken from them.

In their trouble they rightly turn to the Lord as their unfailing resource, and very blessedly they plead His love for their brother, for they say, "He whom Thou lovest is sick" {verse 3}. This, indeed, was true, the Lord loved Lazarus, but we are also told that "Jesus loved Martha, and her sister, and Lazarus" {verse 5}. And as the story proceeds we are permitted to see the way love takes in order to declare, on the one hand, the glory of the Son of God, and, on the other, the compassions of the heart of Jesus.

Further, we again see the difference between these two devoted women. Martha who, on the former occasion, had been cumbered with her service when the Lord of life and glory had visited her house, is now restless and distracted when death has come into the home. Mary who, in the former day, had listened to His word, can now quietly wait for Him to speak and act. Thus we read, "Martha, as soon as she heard that Jesus was coming, went to meet Him: but Mary sat still in the house" {verse 20}. When, however, she received the word, "The Master is come and calleth for thee," she at once acts in obedience to the word, for we read, "She arose quickly, and came unto Him" {verses 28-29}.

"Then when Mary was come where Jesus was, and saw Him, she fell down at His feet" {verse 32}. For the second time this devoted woman is found in the lowly place at the feet of Jesus. The Jews, mistaking her action, say, "She goeth unto the grave to weep there" {verse 31}. She was doing that which is far better, that which faith alone can do; she was going to the feet of Jesus *to weep there*. To weep at the grave of a loved one even the world can do, but it brings no comfort to the sorrowing heart. But to weep at the feet of Jesus is to find the comfort of His love, for we weep at the feet of One who, in His own time, can raise our dead, and, in the meantime, can comfort our hearts. So it came to pass that Mary, who had been at His feet as a learner is now found at His feet as a mourner.

It is noticeable that in this touching scene there is no record of any word spoken by the Lord to Mary. This only we learn that, in the presence of her great sorrow, "Jesus wept" {verse 35}.

The Jews wrongly interpret these tears as being a token of the Lord's love for Lazarus. He did indeed love Lazarus, but there was no need to weep for one that He was about to raise from the dead. It was the sorrow of the living that drew forth the tears of Jesus, as we read, "When Jesus… saw her weeping … He groaned in the spirit, and was troubled," and His trouble found vent in tears, for "Jesus wept" {verses 33-35}.

In the days of old we read of Jehovah that, "He healeth the broken in heart, and bindeth up their wounds" (Psalm 147:3). In order to heal the broken-hearted He became flesh, and shed His tears to dry ours, and broke His heart to bind up our hearts.

And Jesus is still the same — "The same yesterday, and today, and for ever" {Hebrews 13:8}. In our sorrows, and when our loved ones are taken from us, we still learn that our only real and lasting comfort is found in bowing at His feet, and pouring out our sorrow in the presence of the One who once wept with these broken-hearted women.

At His Feet as a Worshipper
Read John 12

The beautiful scene that passes before us in the beginning of the twelfth chapter of John, takes place just six days before the cross. The Lord's devoted life, in which self was ever set aside to serve others in love, draws to its close. At every step of His path He had been dispensing blessing — spreading a feast, as it were, for all the world. Now, at last, a few of His loved ones make a feast for Him, as we read, "There they made Him a supper" {verse 2}.

Christ was in this needy world as a Giver, but it was not often that anyone gave to Him. Once, in the beginning of His way, a few wise men "presented unto Him gifts" and had fallen down and "worshipped Him" {Matthew 2:11}. Now, at the end of His path, they make a supper for Him and, again, one is found at His feet with her gifts as a worshipper.

Truly, too, there had been a moment when Levi had made Him "a great feast in his own house." There the Lord had sat down with "a great company of publicans and others" in order to dispense blessing to sinners {Luke 5:29}. Now

He sits down in company with a few of His own in order to receive the homage of saints.

Christ is the One for Whom they make the supper — the centre of the feast and the Object before every heart. Lazarus, and others, are present, but, we read, they "sat at the table *with Him*" {verse 2}. The supper was *for Him*, and the guests were *"with Him"*. The blessedness, and the greatness, of the occasion was that He, the Son of God, was present.

Again, the two sisters, Martha and Mary, are present. Martha serves, but no longer is she cumbered with her service, or complaining of others. She thinks only of the One for whom they had made the supper. For the third time Mary is found at the feet of the Lord, but no longer to receive His words and His sympathy, but to give to Him the worship of a heart that loved Him, for Mary's gifts, Mary's acts, and Mary's attitude, all breathe the spirit of worship.

Drawn by attachment of heart to Christ she had sat at His feet, listened to His words, and learned something of His mind. Now we see that affection for Christ is the secret of all true service. Moved by this love for Christ she does the right thing at the right moment. She might have left the ointment in the alabaster box and presented it to Christ, but this would not have put the same honour upon Christ. She pours it out upon His feet. She does *the right act*. She might, at some earlier moment in the Lord's life, have anointed His feet with the ointment, but she waits until the hour of His going to the cross and the grave has arrived. Moved by the instincts of love she does the right act *at the right moment*, as the Lord can say, "Against the day of My burying hath she kept this" {verse 7}. Christ was everything to Mary. Christ was her life, and all that she has is devoted to Him. The costly ointment, and the hair of her head — the glory of a woman — are used to put honour upon Christ. She is not even praising Him for all that He had done, or was about to do, but she bows at His feet as a worshipper because of *all that He is*.

Thus acting she puts honour upon the One that the world had rejected and was about to nail to a cross. She forgets herself, and her blessings, and thinks only of Christ. How blessed, if, when we make Him a supper, in a like spirit of worship we could each one pass out of sight of ourselves, and our blessings, and see no man any more save Jesus only and His glory.

Thus acting we should, like Mary in her day, be misunderstood by the world, and even by many true disciples, but we should, also like Mary, have the approval of the Lord. In the eyes of the world her act was mere waste. So in Christendom today, Christianity is viewed merely as a system for making the world a better and a brighter place. The one great aim is to benefit man; all else is waste. In one parable the Lord likens the Kingdom of Heaven to "a King who made a wedding feast for His Son" {Matthew 22:2, N.Tr.}. In the spirit of this parable the disciples had made a supper for the Lord, and Mary had put honour upon Christ. And though the world may condemn, the Lord approves for He says, "Let her alone," and again, in another gospel, He can say, "She hath wrought a good work upon Me" {verse 7; Matthew 26:10}. Indeed, so highly does the Lord appreciate Mary's act that He adds, "Wheresoever this gospel shall be preached in the whole world, there shall also this, that this woman hath done, be told for a memorial of her" (Matthew 26:13).

Moreover, the Lord can say, "Me ye have not always" {verse 8}. It will be our privilege and our joy to worship Him in glory, but it was Mary's privilege, and it is still ours, to worship Him in the world where He is rejected, and in the face of scorn and reproach of men. Mary seized the occasion to render to Him this precious service. As one has said, "She never could have recalled it in eternity ... Love will find new ways of expressing itself to Him then. But it will not be what He looks for from us now. There will be no self to be denied, no cross to be borne, no world to be surrendered, no reproach to be encountered then."[31]

How blessed, too, was the effect of her act of devotion to Christ, for we read, "the house was filled with the odour of the ointment" {verse 3}. Lazarus may hold sweet communion with Christ, and Martha may serve Christ, but Mary's act of worship, that was so precious to the heart of Christ, was also a joy to all that were in the house. That which gives honour to Christ will bring blessing to others.

We may rightly commune with Christ about many things, we may rightly serve Him in many ways, but the worship that makes everything of Christ will surpass all else in the day when we make Him a supper. So will it be in that great day when all the redeemed are gathered home. The new song will be sung, that renders praise to the Lord for all that He has done. Heaven and earth will join to celebrate His glory, but, above all we read of those who "fell down and worshipped Him" {Revelation 5:14}. Beyond all the mighty work that He has done, and beyond all the glory that He has acquired, *He will be worshipped because of all that He is.* Then we shall be able to say,

---

[31] Anon.

AT HIS FEET

The heart is satisfied; can ask no more;
All thought of self is now for ever o'er:
Christ, its unmingled Object, fills the heart
In blest adoring love — its endless part.[32]

---

[32] J. N. Darby, 1872

The Lord Thy Keeper
READ PSALM 121

In this beautiful Psalm we have the experiences of a believer who, in the midst of trials, finds in the Lord his help and unfailing resource. The first verse is really a question. It should read:

> "I will lift up mine eyes unto the mountains: from whence shall my help come?" (verse 1, R.V.)

The God-fearing man finds himself faced with trials and difficulties, but realises that in himself he has no power to meet the circumstances. He needs "help." The greatest source of weakness in the presence of trial is often the self-confidence that leads us to think we can meet the trial in our own strength, or by our own wisdom. We have to learn, and it may be like Peter of old, through bitter experience, that, in the presence of trial and temptation, we have no strength in ourselves. At every step we need a helper to support us in the trial, and carry us through the trial.

Realising his need of help, the question immediately arises in the soul of the Psalmist, "From whence shall my help come?" He is surrounded by mountains that look strong, imposing, and immovable, even as there are those in the world that apparently are firmly established in power, and unassailable by an enemy. But can we trust in any fellow creature? The prophet Jeremiah tells us, "Truly in vain is salvation hoped for from the hills, and from the multitude of mountains: truly in the LORD our God is the salvation of Israel" (Jeremiah 3:23). Realising his need of help, and that the help of man is in vain, the godly man turns from the creature to the Creator, and very blessedly he says,

"My help cometh from the LORD, which made heaven and earth." (verse 2, R.V.)

He does not fall back on the acknowledgement of a general truth that there is help in the LORD, but, in simple personal faith, he says, "*My* help cometh from the LORD."

In the remaining verses of the Psalm the Spirit of God answers this simple faith by unfolding to us the blessings of the one who looks to the LORD for his help. The one recurring thought in these verses is the constant care of the LORD. The word "keep" is the characteristic word of the Psalm. Bearing in mind that the word "preserve," in verses 7 and 8, should be translated "keep," it will be noticed that this encouraging word occurs six times in the last six verses.

HE WILL KEEP US FROM ALL DANGER

"He will not suffer thy foot to be moved." {verse 3, R.V.}

First, the soul learns, that, looking to the LORD for help, he will be kept amidst *all dangers*. In days when we may be faced with sudden dangers, working desolation, how good to be encouraged by the word, "Be not afraid of sudden fear, neither of the desolation of the wicked when it cometh. For the LORD shall be thy confidence, and shall *keep thy foot from being moved*" (Proverbs 3:25-26). If we take our eyes off the LORD, and get occupied with the passing prosperity of the wicked, we may have to say, like the man of Psalm 73, "My feet were almost gone; my steps had well nigh slipped" {verse 2}. Looking to the LORD, and rejoicing in the LORD, we shall be able to say, with Hannah of old, "He will keep the feet of His saints ... for by strength shall no man prevail" (1 Samuel 2:1, 9).

The road we travel may at times be rough, the enemy may oppose with his wiles and snares; temptations may abound, and difficulties arise — all these trials the LORD may allow — but there is one thing He will not allow: He will not suffer the feet of those that trust in Him to be moved from the path that leads to glory. Thus, in the next Psalm, in response to the LORD's word "He will not suffer thy foot to be moved," the godly soul can say with the utmost confidence, "Our feet shall stand within thy gates, O Jerusalem" (Psalm 122:2). The last words of the Lord to Peter were, "Follow Me" {John 21:22}. He has marked out the path for the Christian, and if, with our eye upon Christ as our unfailing help, we follow Him, it will lead far into the depths of glory where He has gone.

> For the path where our Saviour has gone
> Has led up to His Father and God,
> To the place where He's now on the throne,
> And His strength shall be ours on the road.[33]

HIS CARE WILL BE UNCEASING

> "He that keepeth thee will not slumber. Behold He that keepeth Israel shall neither slumber nor sleep." {verses 3-4, R.V.}

Secondly, the one who looks in simple faith to the LORD, learns that His care is *unceasing*. An apostle may sleep on the mount in the presence of a glory too bright for nature; and again in the garden in the presence of a sorrow too deep for our endurance; but the One who is our Keeper

---
[33] J. N. Darby, 1849

will "neither slumber nor sleep." A back-sliding saint, like Jonah of old, may be "fast asleep," even when the LORD is working, the wind is rising, the sea is raging, the ship is sinking, and the men of the world are trembling {Jonah 1:5}, but there is One, who having loved His own which are in the world, loves them unto the end with a love that never ceases to care for His own amid all the storms of life.

> Thou weariest not most gracious Lord,
>   Though we may weary grow;
> In season, the sustaining word
>   Thou giv'st our hearts to know.[34]

HIS HELP IS ALWAYS AVAILABLE

"The LORD is thy keeper: the LORD is thy shade upon thy right hand." {verse 5, R.V.}

Thirdly, looking to the LORD for His help, the soul is assured that the help of the Lord is *always available*. A friend at our right hand is a friend at our side, to whom we can turn at any moment. So David can say, "I have set the LORD alway before me: because He is at my right hand, I shall not be moved" {Psalm 16:8}. The wicked man, trusting in himself, "said in his heart, I shall not be moved," only to come under the judgment of the LORD (Psalm 10:6, 16). The godly man, trusting in the Lord at his right hand, can say, "I shall not be moved." Moreover, he can say it with the utmost confidence, for if the Lord says, "I will never leave thee, nor forsake thee, ... we may boldly say, The Lord is my helper, and I will not fear what man shall do unto me" (Hebrews 13:5-6). How good to realise there is a Friend beside me, to whom I can turn — One with all wisdom to guide in every difficulty, with all the power to overcome every opposition, with all sympathy in every sorrow, and all grace for every weakness, and mercy for every need.

---

[34] M. Bowley

"THE LORD IS MY SHEPHERD"

> The storm may roar without me,
> My heart may low be laid,
> But God is round about me,
> And can I be dismayed?[35]

HE WILL KEEP US AT ALL SEASONS

"The sun shall not smite thee by day, nor the moon by night." {verse 6, R.V.}

Fourthly, the believer looking to the LORD for his help, is assured that he will be kept at *all seasons*. In a world of warring nations we have to face ever present dangers, both "by day" and "by night." The LORD does not say to the believer, "Thou shalt not have to face these terrors even as others," but He says, "If you make Me your 'refuge', and put your 'trust' in Me, 'Thou shalt not be afraid for the terror *by night*; nor for the arrow that flieth *by day*. Nor for the pestilence that walketh in *darkness*; nor for the destruction that wasteth *at noonday*'" (Psalm 91:2, 5-6).

HE WILL KEEP US FROM ALL EVIL

"The LORD shall keep thee from all evil: He shall keep thy soul." {verse 7, R.V.}

Fifthly, the believer that looks to the LORD for his help will be kept from *all evil*. At a time when the world, as in the days of Noah, is increasingly marked by corruption and violence, evil will take many forms. Scripture speaks of evil thoughts, evil imaginations, evil words, evil deeds, and evil doers. The Christian, being blessed with all spiritual blessings in heavenly places, will, in a special way, be opposed by the "spiritual wickedness in high places" that is working behind the scenes. Nevertheless, looking to the LORD, the believer will, "in the power of His might," be able to withstand every attack of the enemy in "the evil day," and thus be kept from evil (Ephesians 6:10-13).

---

[35] A. L. Waring, 1850

Moreover, in a world in which we know not what a day may bring forth how good to know that, of the one who looks to the LORD for his help, it can be said, "He shall not be afraid of *evil tidings*: his heart is fixed, trusting in the LORD" (Psalm 112:7). The Apostle Paul warns us that we live in a day when "*evil men* and seducers shall wax worse and worse, deceiving, and being deceived" (2 Timothy 3:13). In his day he had to meet those who did him "*much evil*", but, trusting in the Lord, he could say, "The Lord shall deliver me from *every evil work*, and will preserve me unto His heavenly kingdom" (2 Timothy 4:14, 18).

> Nought can stay our steady progress,
> More than conquerors we shall be
> If our eyes, whate'er the danger,
> Look to Thee, and none but Thee.[36]

HE WILL KEEP US IN ALL CIRCUMSTANCES

"The LORD shall keep thy going out and thy coming in." {verse 8, R.V.}

Sixthly, the soul that looks to the LORD for his help can count upon the unfailing care of the LORD *in all circumstances*. "Going" and "coming" speak of the changing circumstances that mark a world of unrest. In the gospel day, the Lord could say to His disciples, "Come ye yourselves apart into a desert place, and rest awhile: for there were many *coming* and *going*, and they had not leisure so much as to eat" (Mark 6:31). In His compassionate care the Lord will give us times of rest "apart" from the busy world; but, down here, it will only be "rest awhile" — words that indicate we must be again in movement. For the eternal rest we must look on. "There remaineth ... a rest to the people of God." Of the one that entereth into that blessed rest we read, "He shall

---
[36] W. Williams

"THE LORD IS MY SHEPHERD"

go no more out" (Hebrews 4:9; Revelation 3:12). In the meantime, in all the busy round of a life of toil in a world of need, the one that looks to the Lord for his help can count on the Lord to keep him in every circumstance.

> Wherever He may guide me,
>   No want shall turn me back;
> My Shepherd is beside me,
>   And nothing can I lack,
> His wisdom ever waketh,
>   His sight is never dim;
> He knows the way He taketh,
>   And I will walk with Him.[37]

HE WILL KEEP US THROUGH ALL TIME FOR EVERMORE

"From this time forth and for evermore." {verse 8, R.V.}

Finally, we learn that the one who looks to the Lord for his help may be assured that he will be kept *through all time even for evermore*. The Psalmist, doubtless, had the Millennial reign in view; the Christian can give a wider application to the words as he looks on to a glad eternity to be spent "evermore" with Christ and like Christ in the Father's house, where He has gone to prepare a place for His heavenly people. The Lord can say of His sheep, "I give unto them eternal life; and they shall never perish, neither shall any one pluck them out of My hand" {John 10:28}. In the beautiful picture of Luke 15, the Lord *finds* His lost sheep, "*layeth* it on His shoulders," and "cometh *home*" {verses 5-6}. Nothing less than His home will do for His sheep. We may wander, but He finds His sheep, He keeps them in His strength in their passage through time, and at last He will bring all His wandering sheep home to be, "FOR EVER WITH THE LORD."

We thus learn from this beautiful Psalm that, trusting in the LORD, and looking to Him for our help, we shall find,

---
[37] A. L. Waring, 1850

THE LORD THY KEEPER

- He will keep us from all danger;
- His care will be unceasing;
- His help is always available;
- He will keep us at all seasons;
- He will keep us from all evil;
- He will keep us in all circumstances;
- He will keep us through all time for evermore.

> Oh keep my soul, then, Jesus
> Abiding still with Thee,
> And if I wander, teach me
> Soon back to Thee to flee.[38]

---

[38] J. N. Darby, 1845

The Brokenhearted
READ PSALM 147:2-5; LUKE 4:18

In the fourth chapter of the Gospel of Luke we have the touching record of the Lord's entrance upon His public ministry in this world of sin and sorrow; and we learn, from His own lips, the character of His ministry. Quoting Isaiah's prophecy concerning Himself, He says, "The spirit of the Lord is upon Me, because He hath anointed Me to preach the gospel to the poor; He hath sent me *to heal the brokenhearted*."

The world is full of broken hearts. It may endeavour to cover up its sorrow with a mirth and laughter but, says the preacher, in the book of Proverbs, "Even in laughter the heart is sorrowful" (Proverbs 14:13). Underneath all the outward gaiety of the world there are secret sorrows and broken hearts.

Turning to the word of God, we discover for our comfort that God is not indifferent to these broken hearts. The Psalmist tells us that God is One that "healeth the broken in heart, and bindeth up their wounds" {verse 3}. Moreover, the Psalmist immediately adds, "He telleth the number of the stars; He calleth them all by their names. Great is our Lord" (verses 4-5). The number of the stars is too great for us to tell; the sorrow of a broken heart too deep for us to fathom; but God can count the stars in heaven and heal the broken hearts on earth. In the greatness of His love He gave His only begotten Son to come into this world to heal the brokenhearted.

When we look at Jesus, we at last see One perfect Man who came into this world to seek broken hearts. The devil, indeed, sought to turn Him from His quest, by offering Him all the kingdoms of this world and their glory. But, refusing the world, its honours, and its riches, He chose to become a poor Man seeking brokenhearted men in order to dry their tears, and heal their wounds.

As we trace His path through this valley of tears, in search of broken hearts, we see Him, in the Gospel of Luke, healing the heart of a brokenhearted sinner; binding up the wounds of a brokenhearted saint, and drying the tears of a brokenhearted widow. Moreover, we learn that such was the wickedness and hardness of man's heart that at last His heart was broken. We broke the heart of the One who came to heal our broken hearts.

Thus we discover that hearts are broken by the sins of the sinner, by the failures of the saints, by the death of our loved ones, and above all, by unrequited love.

THE BROKENHEARTED SINNER
READ LUKE 7:36-38

In the touching scene that took place in Simon the Pharisee's house we are permitted to gaze upon that most wonderful sight — a meeting between the Saviour and the sinner. A poor woman who was known in the city as a sinner — and therefore we may conclude a fallen woman — had heard of Jesus. She had heard the people saying that Jesus was, "A Friend of publicans and sinners." She had probably heard, from His own lips, that gracious invitation, "Come unto Me, all ye that labour and are heavy laden, and I will give you rest" {Matthew 11:19, 28}. Weary of her terrible life, with a conscience burdened with her sins, without a friend in the world, she hears of Jesus, the Son of God. She hears that He is the Friend of sinners and that He bids her come.

Driven by her need, and drawn by His grace, she comes to Jesus; and in this fine scene we are permitted to see the result of a sinner coming to the Saviour. She felt that, at all cost, she must get into the presence of this wonderful Saviour. So she enters the Pharisee's house and goes straight to the feet of Jesus. At first no word is spoken, but two things happen, for we read, she "stood at His feet behind Him *weeping*," and she "*kissed* His feet" {verse 38}. Those tears tell of a heart that is broken; those kisses of a heart that is won.

What was it that broke her heart? What was it that won her heart? Was it not that she saw her life, with all its sins, in the presence of His heart with all its love and grace? She discovered that His grace was greater than her sins, and that though He knew the worst about her, yet He loved her, and did not drive her away or utter one word of reproach. She could hold out against the scorn of men, and the sneers of the Pharisee, but such love as this broke her heart. It is not the badness of man, but the goodness of God that leads to repentance (Romans 2:4).

Having broken her heart by His grace He binds up her heart with His words of love, for, He says, "Thy sins are forgiven ... thy faith hath saved thee; go in peace" (verses 48-50).

The way of this brokenhearted woman is still the way of blessing for any poor sinner.

First we are made conscious of our sins and need.

Secondly, God in His grace brings us the good news of the only One who can meet our need. We hear of the Saviour who came into the world to save sinners, who has given "Himself a ransom for all", and "offered Himself without spot to God", and so satisfied God by His mighty work on the cross, that God can proclaim forgiveness to a world of sinners, and invite whosoever will to believe in Jesus {1 Timothy 2:6; Hebrews 9:14}.

Thirdly, we learn that believing in Him we may know on the authority of God's word that our sins are forgiven and our souls saved (Acts 11:20-21; 10:43).

Blessed moment when having learned our need and heard of Jesus we believe and turn to Him, to find ourselves alone in His presence, conscious of our sins but realising that, in spite of knowing all our sins, He loves us. Such love will break our hearts and win them for ever.

THE BROKENHEARTED SAINT
READ LUKE 22:54-62

We have looked at a brokenhearted sinner in the house of Simon the Pharisee; now we are permitted to see a brokenhearted backslider in the house of the high priest. We may truly have our sins forgiven, and love the Lord with all the ardour and sincerity of the Apostle Peter, and yet, but for the grace of the Lord, we may, like the Apostle, break down and deny the Lord. Through storm and sunshine this devoted servant had followed hard after his Master during the years of His wonderful ministry; but there comes a day when he *"followed afar off"* {verse 54}. Walking at a distance from his Master he is soon found in the company of the enemies of his Master. So we read that when the enemies of the Lord "had kindled a fire," and "were set down together," that "Peter sat down among them" {verse 55}. Sitting among the Lord's enemies it is not long before he enters into temptation. It seemed, indeed, only a small temptation for it comes from "a certain maid." Alas! away from the Lord, in bad association, a very little thing is sufficient to trip us up. The maid may be weak enough, but she has poor Peter at an advantage for she saw him "as he sat by the fire." All she says is, "This man was also with Him" {verse 56}. Peter scents danger, so without hesitation, the man who in his self-confidence had said, "I am ready to go with Thee, both into prison, and to death," flatly denies the Lord, saying, "Woman, I know Him not" {Luke 22:33, 57}.

Three times he denies the Lord, and then, according to the words of the Lord "The cock crew." Peter has denied the Lord; but has the Lord's heart changed toward Peter? Blessed be His Name, His love is an unchanging love; "Having loved His own which were in the world, He loved them unto the end" {John 13:1}. So it came to pass, that at the very moment when Peter turned from the Lord, the Lord turned to Peter, for we read, "the Lord turned, and looked upon Peter" {verse 61}. We may grieve His heart but we cannot change His love. We may be sure that that look was a look of infinite love that seemed to say to Peter, "You have denied Me, Peter, you have said that you do not know Me, but in spite of all your denials I love you."

What was the effect of that look? It broke the heart of the poor backsliding Peter; for we read, "Peter went out, and wept bitterly" {verse 62}. Like the fallen sinner of Luke 7, the backsliding saint of Luke 22, sees his sins in the light of the Lord's love; and the love that rose above his sins broke his heart.

We know, too, on the resurrection day, the tender way love took to heal this brokenhearted man and drive away his tears. So in all our backslidings, He restores our souls, by breaking our hearts and winning our hearts with His unchanging love.

THE BROKENHEARTED WIDOW
READ LUKE 7:11-15

The story of the brokenhearted widow reminds us that over the fairest scenes of this world there lies the dark shadow of death. Nain means "pleasant," and the situation of the city was beautiful, but death was there. Then for our comfort we learn that into this world of death the Lord of life had come, and not alone with power to raise the dead, but with the love and sympathy that can feel for us in our sorrows, dry our tears, and heal the brokenhearted. So "it came to pass" that Jesus went into the city of Nain, and "His disciples went with Him and much people" {verse 11}. This company with the Lord of life in the midst, meets another company with a dead body in the midst; for, as the Lord came nigh to the city, "a dead man was carried out, the only son of his mother, and she was a widow: and much people of the city was with her" {verse 12}. How beautiful is the way the Lord takes to heal her broken heart. Moved with compassion, He first dries her tears, and then removes the cause of her sorrow. Had we the power we should probably have first raised the dead, and then said to the woman, "Weep no more." But Jesus takes another way — a better way — that makes the story so full of comfort for us all. He first says to the brokenhearted mother, "Weep not," and then He raises the dead {verse 13}. Thus the woman would have been able to say, "In my great sorrow He came so near to me, that He wiped away my tears. He not only took me out of my sorrowful circumstances, but He walked beside me *in them*." Thus He shows by His compassion and sympathy that He can wipe away our tears, before He raises our dead. This suits our case, for

Jesus is gone, and He does not yet raise our loved ones when taken from us; but He speaks comfort to our broken hearts, and dries our tears, while we wait for the day when He will raise our loved ones who have fallen asleep in Jesus. His compassions go before His mercies. We have the comfort of His love while we wait for the display of His resurrection power. Then indeed, that word will be fulfilled, "God shall wipe away all tears ... and there shall be no more death" {Revelation 21:4}.

> A few short years and all is o'er,
> Your sorrow, pain, will soon pass by;
> Then lean in faith on God's dear Son,
> He'll wipe the tear from every eye.[39]

THE BROKENHEARTED SAVIOUR
READ LUKE 19:41-48

We have seen that our sins, and our backslidings, seen in the light of His love can break our hearts, and that death can cast its shadow over the fairest scene and break our hearts. But in this touching scene on the Mount of Olives we see a yet deeper sorrow — the sorrow of unrequited love. We at times may have our hearts broken by unrequited love, but, even as the Saviour's love rises above all other loves, so, when His love is flung back in His face, He feels, in measure beyond all others, the sorrow of unrequited love. The depth of His sorrow can only be measured by the height of His love.

So we read, "When He was come near, He beheld the city, and wept over it" {verse 41}. His love had been lavished on these poor people, but they only rewarded Him evil for good, and hatred for His love (Psalm 109:5). When He told them that He had come to heal the brokenhearted, they were "filled with wrath, and rose up, and thrust Him out of the city" {Luke 4:16-29}. When He forgave sins,

---
[39] Mrs Mackinlay, about 1850

they charged Him with blasphemy {Luke 5:20-21}. When He healed a poor cripple, they were filled with madness {Luke 6:6-11}. When He received poor sinners, and ate with them, they said He was a gluttonous man and a wine-bibber {Luke 7:34}. When He goes to raise a dead girl, they laugh Him to scorn {Luke 8:49-54}; and when He delivers a man from the devil they say, "He casteth out devils through Beelzebub the chief of the devils" {Luke 11:14-15}.

They opened their mouths against Him, they spoke against Him with a lying tongue, and fought against Him without cause, and for His love they were His enemies (Psalm 109:2-5). Nevertheless, man's heartless treatment drew forth no expression of indignation from Christ, no bitter and revengeful word fell from His lips. "When He was reviled, He reviled not again [and] when He suffered He threatened not" {1 Peter 2:23}. The hardness of our hearts only called forth a sorrow that found expression in His tears. We broke His heart at last, for He could say, "I am poor and needy, and my heart is wounded within me." And having broken His heart we sought to "slay the broken in heart" (Psalm 109:16, 22). So we read "the chief priests and the scribes and the chief of the people sought to destroy Him" {Luke 19:47}. What a scene! Outside the city, the heartbroken Saviour weeping over sinners: inside, hardened sinners seeking to destroy the Saviour — seeking to shed the blood of the One who shed His tears over them.

In yet a little while there will be a glorious answer to those tears for very soon He will be surrounded by a great host of brokenhearted sinners saved by grace and backsliding saints restored by grace, in a scene where "God shall wipe away all tears from their eyes; and there shall be no more death, neither sorrow, nor crying, neither shall there be any more pain: for the former things are passed away." Then, "He shall see of the travail of His soul, and shall be satisfied" {Revelation 21:4; Isaiah 53:11}.

> I cannot tell how silently He suffered,
>   As with His peace He graced this place of tears,
> Or how His heart upon the cross was broken,
>   The crown of pain to three-and-thirty years.
> But this I know, He heals the brokenhearted,
>   And stays our sin and calms our lurking fear,
> And lifts the burden from the heavy laden,
>   For yet the Saviour, Saviour of the world is here.[40]

---

[40] W. Y. Fullerton, c.1920

"THE LORD IS MY SHEPHERD"

Other Books by Hamilton Smith from Scripture Truth Publications

UNDERSTANDING THE NEW TESTAMENT Series

The Gospel of Mark: An Expository Outline

> ISBN 978-0-901860-69-9; (paperback)
> ISBN 978-0-901860-70-5; (hardback)
> 144 pages; March 2007

The Epistle to the Romans: An Expository Outline

> ISBN 978-0-901860-85-9; (paperback)
> 196 pages; June 2008

The Epistle to the Colossians: An Expository Outline

> ISBN 978-0-901860-90-3; (paperback)
> 68 pages; June 2009

UNDERSTANDING THE OLD TESTAMENT Series

Elijah: A Prophet of the Lord

> ISBN 978-0-901860-68-2; (paperback)
> 80 pages; March 2007

Elisha: The Man of God

> ISBN 978-0-901860-79-8; (paperback)
> 92 pages; March 2007

God, Israel, Idolatry and Christ: A Brief Exposition of Isaiah 40 to 57

> ISBN 978-0-901860-98-9; (paperback)
> 80 pages; September 2018

UNDERSTANDING CHRISTIANITY Series

Short Papers on the Church

> ISBN 978-0-901860-80-4; (paperback)
> 96 pages; March 2008

"THE LORD IS MY SHEPHERD"

GLEANINGS FROM THE PAST SERIES

EXTRACTS FROM THE LETTERS OF SAMUEL RUTHERFORD

ISBN 978-0-901860-81-1; (paperback)
96 pages; March 2008

EXTRACTS FROM THE WRITINGS OF WILLIAM GURNALL

ISBN 978-0-901860-82-8; (paperback)
100 pages; August 2008

EXTRACTS FROM THE WRITINGS OF THOMAS WATSON

ISBN 978-0-901860-83-5; (paperback)
96 pages; April 2009

www.ingramcontent.com/pod-product-compliance
Lightning Source LLC
Chambersburg PA
CBHW060158050426
42446CB00013B/2894